This book is for you if

- you want to reflect on the big questions of life - suffering, injustice, faith;

- you find the Old Testament a bit unwieldy and want a straightforward way into one of the most powerful books in the Bible;

- you want a way to read Job in a week;

- you want to have a fascinating evening in a home group;

- you wish to hold a theological seminar on this key aspect of OT Wisdom;

- you want to put on a public drama event, e.g. on a Sunday evening in church, to which you can invite people from neighbouring churches.

- you enjoy the wonderful engravings of William Blake.

What they say about Rev Andy's books

Bible in Brief
"There has never been a sustained and powerful renewal of Christian faith without a renewed engagement with the Bible. Andy Roland provides a practical introduction to a lifetime relationship with the word of God."
Rt Revd Richard Chartres, former Bishop of London

"This book does what few others do - it offers a very helpful guide for those looking for a brief overview of the Bible and its story."
Rt Revd Graham Tomlin, Bishop of Kensington

"I wish I had read this book fifty years ago. Andy Roland paints with a broad brush, and shows how the different parts of the Bible relate to each other. He tackles difficult subjects with both brevity and clarity. Key passages in Scripture are identified, and helpful questions asked about each to aid reflection. An excellent brief account of the Bible story and its importance today."
Dr James Behrens, barrister

Discovering Psalms as Prayer
"In 'Discovering Psalms as Prayer' Andy Roland weaves together the wisdom of a faithful, personal pilgrimage with practical guidance for reading the psalms. It will be a gift to those wanting to make that discovery for themselves. We are in his debt."
from foreword by Revd David Runcorn, author of
Spirituality Workbook, Choice, Desire and the Will of God etc.

A Week of Prayer in Jerusalem

"Andy Roland relates his experiences at the grass roots in Jerusalem during last year's 2017 Week of Prayer for Christian Unity. And to those contemplating their first visit to the Holy Land, this book will allow them to soak up some of the atmosphere in advance. Outside of the appendices which are themselves informative and well worth reading, the author has adopted a diary style, peppered with pictures…This is one traveller's tale that is well worth getting hold of."

John Singleton, Methodist Recorder

Five Steps to Faith

A pastoral response to families seeking baptism for their children if they don't know the Christian story.

"Great material here" Canon Mark Collinson,
Director of School of Mission, Winchester

"I hope the book spreads far and wide & proves useful to many!"
Rt Revd Graham Tomlin, Bishop of Kensington

Look inside all the books at bibleinbrief.org

THE BOOK OF JOB

arranged for private reading,
group discussion
& public performance
by Rev Andy Roland

Foreword by Bishop Rowan Williams

Published by Filament Publishing Ltd
16, Croydon Road, Waddon, Croydon Surrey CR0 4PA

The right of Andrew Roland to be identified as the author of this work has been asserted by him in accordance with the Designs and Copyright Act 1988

© Andrew Roland 2019

Printed by IngramSpark

ISBN 978-1-913192-50-1

Second Edition

New Revised Standard Version Bible, copyright 1989, Division of Christian Education of the National Council of the Churches of Christ in the United States of America. Used by permission.
All rights reserved.

The book is protected by international copyright and may not be copied in anyway without the prior written permission of the publishers.

Contents

Foreword by Rowan Williams	8
Introducing Job	9
Job for Private Reading	18
Job for Group Study	20

The Book of Job for Group Study   **23**

Putting on Job as a Public Performance	43
Musical Interludes	45

The Book of Job for Public Performance   **47**

The Beginning	48
Introduction	49
First Cycle	53
Second Cycle	65
Third Cycle	75
God Speaks	85
The Ending	89
The Conclusion	91

Afterword: The Meaning of Job   **93**

Bibliography	112

Foreword

One of the most damaging myths about religious faith is that it stifles honest questioning and simply demands unthinking assent. Yet the fact is that, from the Book of Job to Christian poets and mystics like John of the Cross or George Herbert, from the writer of the psalms to Frank Cottrell Boyce's searing play, God on Trial, believers have not only felt free to express their anger and doubt, but have believed that their faith itself licenses them to express it. The great Anglican writer Charles Williams said about the Book of Job that it showed us a God who had made human beings precisely to ask difficult questions.

To understand anything about how the book works, we need to hear it as drama, as an exchange of passionate, difficult speeches. Hence the importance of this 'arrangement', which allows us to enter the space of the writer's imagination and the writer's faith as it is tested, pushed and squeezed, almost rejected, revived, articulated in intense protest and equally intense trust. For Christians, the ultimate response to Job is in the record of the God who stands with us in our suffering in the life and death of Jesus Christ; God's communication to the world, God's Word, becomes flesh and blood. Presenting the drama of Job in this way helps us take a small step towards understanding this, as the words become more obviously the flesh and blood exchanges of real people.

Rowan Williams
Magdalen College, Cambridge

Introducing Job

What is Job?

The Book of Job is one of the longest books in the Bible, equivalent to each of Genesis, Exodus, the Histories, the major Prophets and each of the Gospels. It is unique in the Bible in the way it explores just one major question - how can we make sense of suffering?

However, it is not unique in the literature of the Ancient Near East. The struggle to make sense of suffering and injustice has exercised the minds of men and women from the dawn of history. About 2000 BCE "A Dispute about Suicide" was written in Egypt.

> To whom shall I speak today?
> Men are contented with evil,
> Goodness is neglected everywhere...
> To whom shall I speak today?
> I am laden with misery
> Through lack of a friend....

Some time between 1400 and 1000 BCE a dialogue was written in Babylon, in modern day Iraq, called the Babylonian Theodicy. Here is an extract:

Sufferer	Just one word would I put before you: Those who neglect the god go the way of prosperity, while those who pray to the goddess are impoverished and dispossessed. In my youth I sought the will of my god with prostration and prayer I followed my goddess, but I was bearing profitless forced labour as a yoke. My god decreed, instead of wealth, destitution.
Friend	The godless cheat who has wealth, a death-dealing weapon pursues him. Unless you seek the will of the god, what luck have you?

> *He that bears his god's yoke never lacks food,*
> *though it be sparse.*
> *Seek the kindly wind of the gods;*
> *What you have lost over a year,*
> *you will make up in a moment.*

Similar writings in the Ancient Near East include the Sumerian Job, the Babylonian Job, the Epic of Gilgamesh and the Egyptian Story of the Eloquent Peasant. The Bible contains examples of the same struggle in the Psalms and in Ecclesiastes.

> *As for me, me feet had almost stumbled,*
> *my feet had nearly slipped.*
> *For I was envious of the arrogant;*
> *I saw the prosperity of the wicked…*
> *When I thought how to understand this,*
> *it seemed to me a wearisome task…*
>
> (Psalm 73.2-3,16)

> There is no enduring remembrance of the wise or of fools, seeing that in the days to come all will have been long forgotten. How can the wise die just like fools? So I hated life, because what is done under the sun was grievous to me; for all is vanity and a chasing after wind.
>
> (Ecclesiastes 2.16-17)

The problem of Monotheism

The desire to find meaning in injustice and suffering is universal. But the problem is made more acute once you come to believe that there is a unified source of spiritual and creative energy which pervades and rules the universe (God). If you believe that this world is the playground of differing, sometimes warring, spiritual forces (gods), then you have the hope that, if you are suffering, you only have to find the right god to appeal to. An example is this Sumerian prayer from a 7th century BCE Assyrian royal library:

> *O god whom I know or do not know,*
> *my transgressions are many, great are my sins.*
> *O goddess whom I know or do not know,*

> *my transgressions are many, great are my sins.*
> *The transgressions which I have committed, indeed I do not know.*
> *The sin which I have done, indeed I do not know....*
> *The god in the rage of his heart confronted me.*
> *The goddess was angry, she made me become ill....*
> *I utter laments, but no one hears me.*
> *I am troubled; I am overwhelmed; I cannot see.*
> *O my god, merciful one, I address to thee the prayer,*
> *"Ever incline to me."*
> *I kiss the feet of the goddess; I crawl before thee...*

Once you see reality as a unified whole, with the Great Spirit (as Native Americans say) being in charge, then the experience of suffering becomes a major problem. I discuss this in the Afterword "The Meaning of Job" at the end of the book.

Who was Job?

Job was a legendary figure of godliness and righteousness, well before the Bible came to be written. The prophet Ezekiel mentioned him about 590 BCE, during the exile in Babylon:

> *The word of the Lord came to me: Mortal, when a land sins against me by acting faithlessly, and I stretch out my hand against it, and break its staff of bread and send famine upon it, and cut off from it human beings and animals, even if Noah, Daniel, and Job, these three, were in it, they would save only their own lives by their righteousness, says the Lord God...*
>
> (Ezekiel 14.12-14)

This is the same Noah as in Genesis 6 - 9. Daniel is actually Dan'el, a legendary king of Ugarit, and Job came from Uz, or Edom, i.e. none of them were Hebrews or Israelites.

The action of the Book of Job takes place in ancient times, with Job being a figure like Abraham, a patriarch whose wealth was counted in sheep and cattle. Job and his family lived a semi-nomadic lifestyle, with his children commuting from house to house. He also acted as priest to his family:

> *"Job would send and sanctify (his children) according to the number of them, and he would rise early in the morning and offer burnt-offerings according to the number of them all..."*
>
> (Job 1.5)

This echoes what is recorded of Noah after the flood:

> *Then Noah built an altar to the Lord, and took of every clean animal and of every clean bird, and offered burnt-offerings on the altar."*
>
> (Genesis 8.20)

It is remarkable that the person whom the Bible takes as an instance of a perfectly righteous man is neither Jewish nor Hebrew nor an Israelite. He came from Uz, another name for Edom:

> *Rejoice and be glad, O daughter of Edom,*
> *you that live in the land of Uz.*
>
> (Lamentations 4.21)

Edom was in the south of present-day Jordan, south of the Dead Sea. The famous tourist site of Petra is there. Edomites were seen as cousins by Jews because they had a common ancestor through Abraham's son Isaac. But as the Arab proverbs goes, "Relatives are scorpions". Rebekah, Isaac's wife, had twin sons, Esau and Jacob (later named Israel). Being the elder by a few minutes, Esau got all the privileges of the first-born. But Jacob (meaning 'deceiver') manipulated things so that he got those privileges for himself. This brought about a long-standing history of enmity between Hebrews and Edomites. In the 11th century BCE King David *"killed eighteen thousand Edomites in the Valley of Salt. He put garrisons in Edom... and all the Edomites became his servants."* (2 Samuel 8.13-14). When Judah was defeated by Babylon, the Edomites took their revenge. In Psalm 83 they are first among the enemies of Judah: Edom, Ishmael, Moab, Hagrites (east of Gilead), Gebal, Ammon, Amalek, Philistia and Assyria. And yet clearly the righteous Job was an Edomite!

We are told that Job was "blameless and upright", that he owned "7,000 sheep, 3,000 camels, 500 pairs of oxen, 500 donkeys and very many servants." He was "the greatest of all the people of the east" - seen from Israel's perspective this would include all of Babylonia and Sumeria, i.e. the lands from which Abraham came from originally - Ur of the Chaldees and Haran in modern-day Iraq.

Job , we guess, is based on a real person in antiquity, perhaps around 2000 BCE. But in the Book of Job he is used as a typically righteous person, in much the same way as we might introduce King Arthur into a modern book. It makes not an iota of difference to the value of the book which bears his name.

Who wrote Job?

No one knows who wrote the Book of Job, or when, or where. But there are some clues.

First, Job is composed of two distinct elements.

Chapters 1, 2 and 42 are written in prose, not poetry. They use extraordinary numbers to indicate Job's wealth, and place him in a semi-nomadic society. There are scenes in the court of heaven, where the "satan" or accuser suggests that Job's righteous life is not disinterested.

(The satan is actually one of the Lord's courtiers, a prosecuting counsel, similar to the Vatican's 'Devil's Advocate', whose job is to find reasons why someone should not be proclaimed a saint. In Job the word is always used with the definite article 'the'; i.e. he is not meant to be the personal devil of later Jewish and particularly Christian theology. But all the English translations with one exception leave out the article, making him a personal embodiment of evil and relegating the real meaning, 'the accuser', to a footnote. This is unfortunate.)

These first two chapters come from a long-standing oral tradition, which could be subtitled 'Job the Patient'. It was probably set down in writing in the southern kingdom of Judah. We can assume this, because only in these chapters is God is referred to as 'the LORD' or Yahweh. The latter was the probable pronunciation of the name 'Jehovah' and is used in the Roman Catholic Jerusalem Bible. Most translations use the title 'LORD'. This follows the practice of early Jewish rabbis who thought the name was too holy to be pronounced. So they took the vowel signs and fitted them into different consonants to make the Hebrew word for 'Lord', 'Adonai'.

This is used in almost all English versions. It is written in capital letters to indicate that it is a mistranslation!

We can also assume that the main dialogues, chapters 3 to 41, which could be sub-titled "Job the Impatient", came from the northern, wealthier kingdom of Israel. This is because the ancient words for God - El, Eloah or Shaddai (Almighty) - are always used. The sole exceptions are 12.9 and 28.28, (but the latter is certainly a later insertion). The Book of Psalms illustrates this distinction. It is a compilation of various psalm collections, mostly from Judah, using the word "Yahweh" or LORD"; but Book 2 and half of Book 3, Psalms 42 to 83, would have come from Israel, as they typically use the words God or Almighty. This is clear in two otherwise identical psalms, 14 (from Book 1) and 53 (from Book 2)

> *The Lord looks down from heaven on humankind*
> *to see if there are any who are wise,*
> *who seek after God.*
>
> (Psalm 14.2)

> *God looks down from heaven on humankind*
> *to see if there are any who are wise,*
> *who seek after God.*
>
> (Psalm 53.2)

In Psalms 42 to 83 God is consistently referred to as "El" or "Elohim", (God), unlike the rest of the Psalms where the word "Yahweh" is used. So it is clear to me therefore that the main dialogue of Job, chapters 3 to 41, originated in the northern kingdom of Israel, or from a continuing Israelite community in exile if such existed.

When was Job written?

It would, I think, have been possible for Job to have been written during the time of the kingdoms of Judah and Israel. A literary tradition was started under David; the story of David and Bathsheba and the ensuing civil wars is probably a contemporary account. This literary tradition was given a boost by King Solomon when he married an Egyptian princess and imported aspects of Pharaoh's court. So, as in Egypt, an important court official throughout the time of the kingdoms was the secretary or scribe. The northern kingdom of Israel was wealthier and more powerful than Judah, and there is no reason why it could not have produced its own version of the dialogues about suffering which were popular at that time.

However, all the scholars I have read place it after the exile in Babylon, some time between 600 and 300 BCE. This is based on two arguments. First, the language uses Aramaic and Arabian idioms, though more of them in the later Elihu section. For instance, "'or" means light in Hebrew; but in two verses in Job (24.14, 38.24) it has the probable Aramaic dialect meaning 'of evening' or 'west wind', (though translators tend to break the parallelism in 38.24 and translate it as 'light'). However, Aramaic was known during the time of the kingdoms. When the Assyrian army was besieging Jerusalem in 601 BCE, their commander insisted on asking the city to surrender in Hebrew, although the Judaean royal officials asked him to speak in Aramaic because they understood it while the common people did not. (2 Kings 18.26)

The other argument is that the theology of Job presupposes later development. Well, perhaps. But at least part of the book of Proverbs goes back to the time of the kingdoms, because it includes a passage, Proverbs 22.17-29, taken from an ancient Egyptian book of wisdom, the "Instruction of Amen-em-opet"; and Proverbs 25 - 29 were compiled in the reign of King Hezekiah (739 - 682 BCE). Is it really so different from the theology of, say, Amos and Jeremiah?

There are a couple of passages which were almost certainly put in at a later date, chapters 28 and 32 - 37. This will be discussed in the next section. Job had to be written in time for these to be added, before the Hebrew scriptures were translated into Greek in the 2nd century, i.e. well before 150 BCE.

This is a very long way of saying that we don't know who wrote Job, or where or when. And it absolutely does not matter.

The later additions

Job, though long, has a clear structure There is a prologue and an epilogue. In between are three cycles of speeches of Job and his three friends. Then God speaks. This is the structure:

THE BOOK OF JOB

Introductory story	Chapter 1 & 2
Job's complaint and first cycle of speeches	Chapters 3 - 14
Second cycle of speeches	Chapters 15 - 21
Third cycle of speeches	Chapter 22 - 31*
God speaks	Chapters 38 - 41
Epilogue	Chapter 42

*In the third cycle the friends only have one and a half speeches instead of three. The text may have got disrupted. I have lifted most of Job's speech in chapter 27 and given it to Zophar. This is for dramatic purposes, not textual ones.

Chapter 28 is clearly out of place in Job. It is a stand-alone poem about wisdom, and a magnificent one. Definitely worth reading but not as part of Job.

In chapters 32-37 a new character enters the fray, a young man called Elihu the Buzite, perhaps a descendant of a nephew of Abraham (Genesis 22.20-21). He is not mentioned in either the prologue or the epilogue, he merely repeats the arguments that have already been made. There are more Aramaisms than in the rest of the book. It is almost certainly a later insertion. So I leave it out, though I talk about it in the essay "The Meaning of Job" at the end.

Shortening Job

Even with later insertions removed, Job is still a mammoth work, made up of 36 chapters. Definitely too long to read at one sitting. I first put on a public performance of Job for St John's Kingston-upon-Thames in the 1990s. This meant photocopying, scissors and paste. It is much easier now with a computer! I reduced the number of verses by about 50%, first by omitting the passages probably inserted later, then by taking out passages which are difficult for modern audience to understand, and by clarifying the arguments being presented. I tried to keep a balance between the speeches of Job and of his three friends. The result was a performance edition which enables the work to be presented, with musical interludes, in one and a quarter hours. The verse numbering has been left in so that people can make their own adjustments if they wish. The translation used is the New Revised Standard Version, one of the most accurate of modern translations and, while using gender-neutral phrases as far as possible, it does retain a sense of poetry.

In 2015 I joined the congregation of HTB Queens Gate, part of the parish of Holy Trinity Brompton. They have a fortnightly Bible discussion group, and I was asked to lead one session on Job, which I did on Shrove Tuesday 2018. So I had to shorten the book by a further 50%. This makes the speeches quite short, but the basic structure is still there, and it is feasible for any small group to read it through with their existing members. Most of the difficult place names have been left out. In place of the musical interludes, each cycle ends with a short silence of one or two minutes as a breather. It all takes half an hour, leaving ample time for group discussion.

My hope is that these versions will introduce a number of seekers, (and we are all fundamentally seekers), to the astonishingly rigorous and honest arguments of not just one of the greatest books in the Bible, but of world literature.

Note on illustrations

William Blake did a set of water colours illustrating the Book of Job in 1806 and 1821. In 1823 technical improvements in steel engraving for books, using the technology for printing banknotes, made it possible to create much sharper images, and along with Constable and Turner, William Blake produced a set of 22 engraved prints in 1826, again illustrating the Book of Job. All the illustrations in this book are taken from that series of engravings. See Wikipedia on William Blake's "*Illustrations of the Book of Job*".

THE BOOK OF JOB

Job for Private Reading

The obvious way to get to know the book of Job is to start reading it. But there is a problem. If you decided to read one chapter a day, it would take you six weeks, even if you never missed a day. And if you take my suggestion of omitting the (presumed) later insertions, that would still leave 36 chapters, i.e. five weeks, or more than a month. You might feel that there are other parts of the Bible which you should include in your spiritual diet during this period.

This book offers you two possibilities:

Job in one sitting

You could probably get an overview of the book in 20 minutes by sitting down in an armchair with a cup of tea or coffee and reading through the version of Job for group study. You will get a hang of the book, though obviously you miss out on some of the arguments and the poetry.

Job in a week

If, like me, you try to read a passage from the Bible each day, Job fits perfectly into a week's reading. Because there are three cycles of speeches, plus introduction, God's speech and the conclusion, that gives six days of readings which feels doable. You could use the version of Job designed for public performance, which has been shortened but less drastically than the version for group study. It means that each day you would be reading the equivalent of two to five chapters per day, with day 2 being the longest. A serious commitment but not impossible.

After reading each passage, I recommend you have a two minutes' pause and then reflect on the question which is provided for each day. Here is a suggested scheme:

Monday   **Introduction**   **ch. 1 & 2**
- What makes a person "blameless and upright"?
- When tragedy or disaster strike, how have you or people you know reacted?

Tuesday   **First cycle**   **ch. 3 to 13, ed.**
- What might it feel like to think that death is preferable to life?
- What could lead us to think like that?
- Does God protect those who live faithfully?

Wednesday   **Second cycle**   **ch. 14 to 21, ed.**
- Is God sometimes cruel?
- Do bad people get their comeuppance?

Thursday   **Third cycle**   **ch. 22 to 31, ed.**
- Where is God when he is silent?
- What are the signature actions of a righteous person?

Friday   **God's Speaks**   **ch. 38 & 39, ed.**
- When you consider the wonder fo the universe, (e.g. the 2 trillion galaxies), does that lead towards or away from worship of the Eternal One?
- Is death part of the natural order?

Saturday   **Conclusion**   **ch. 42**
- Was Job right to repent?
- What did the three friends do wrong?
- How would Job's memory of his sufferings still affect him after his fortunes had revived?

Sunday   **Poem on wisdom**   **ch. 28**
- Be ready to receive some wisdom today - and note it down.

Note: The Book of Job for Group Study and the Book of Job for Public Performance have been set in two different typefaces, Avenir Next and Palatino, to help with navigating whichever version you want to be on.

THE BOOK OF JOB

Job for Group Study

I am of the generation when being a Christian and church member typically meant church on Sunday and a house group during the week. This was where we could express our opinions, air our doubts and make friends or significant acquaintances. Our 24/7 culture today makes this more tricky, and the pressure on housing makes regular meetings in people's homes more problematic. But it still happens, though it may mean meeting in a church vestry or a room in a community centre.

As I mentioned in "Introducing Job", I had the opportunity to lead one session of my church's fortnightly Bible discussion group on Job. I realised that to use the whole of my version of Job for Public Performance would be far too long for a group session. There would be barely any time for discussion, which is the chief value of these events. (As someone once said: 'I hear, I forget; I see, I remember; I do, I understand'). So I reduced the number of verses by a further 45% and took out as many difficult Hebrew names as possible. I left out the musical interludes, which do not work so well in an informal setting, substituting periods of silence of one or two minutes, so as to have a breather but not to lose the forward momentum. It worked well.

Although it is a drama, it does not need any acting or memorising. You only need six or seven people who are competent at reading aloud. The only person who needs to be chosen with some care is the person reading the part of Job. Clearly, in the original all the speakers are male. It has been my practice to have men read Job and two of the friends, and for women to read the two narrators and the middle friend Bildad. God can of course be of any gender, race or orientation. Narrator 1 tells of the events on earth, Narrator 2 of the events in heaven. You still need a pause for breath after each cycle. I suggest a silence of one or two minutes. This needs to be announced beforehand and a timekeeper appointed, otherwise it is easy to get fidgety and wonder if the silence is ever going to end.

After the half hour of reading, here are some questions which could spark of a group discussion:

Questions for Group Discussion

1 What are Job's accusation against God. Are they valid?

2 How well do Job's friends defend God?

3 How does God respond? Do you know, either personally or by report, of any similar instances?

4 Do things always end up like the ending of the book of Job?

Buying Job

Obviously buying multiple copies of any book gets expensive, especially if it is not going to be used often. So the publisher, Filament Publishing Ltd., is happy to offer the book at a substantial discount if six or more copies are ordered at the same time.

The Book of Job

for Group Study

THE BOOK OF JOB

Narrator 1
There was once a man in the land of Uz whose name was Job. That man was blameless and upright, one who feared God and turned away from evil. ²There were born to him seven sons and three daughters. ³He had seven thousand sheep, three thousand camels, five hundred yoke of oxen, five hundred donkeys, and very many servants; so that this man was the greatest of all the people of the east.

Narrator 2
⁶One day the heavenly beings came to present themselves before the Lord, and Satan also came among them. ⁷The Lord said to Satan, 'Where have you come from?' Satan answered the Lord, 'From going to and fro on the earth, and from walking up and down on it.' ⁸The Lord said to Satan, 'Have you considered my servant Job? There is no one like him on the earth, a blameless and upright man who fears God and turns away from evil.' ⁹Then Satan answered the Lord, 'Does Job fear God for nothing? ¹⁰Have you not put a fence around him and his house and all that he has, on every side? You have blessed the work of his hands, and his possessions have increased in the land. ¹¹But stretch out your hand now, and touch all that he has, and he will curse you to your face.' ¹²The Lord said to Satan, 'Very well, all that he has is in your power; only do not stretch out your hand against him!' So Satan went out from the presence of the Lord.

Narrator 1
¹³One day when his sons and daughters were eating and drinking wine in the eldest brother's house, ¹⁴a messenger came to Job and said, 'The oxen were ploughing and the donkeys were feeding beside them, ¹⁵and the Sabeans fell on them and carried them off, and killed the servants with the edge of the sword; I alone have escaped to tell you.' ¹⁷While he was still speaking, another came and said, 'The Chaldeans formed three columns, made a raid on the camels and carried them off, and killed the servants with the edge of the sword; I alone have escaped to tell you.' ¹⁸While he was still speaking, another came and said, 'Your sons and daughters were eating and drinking wine in their eldest brother's house, ¹⁹and suddenly a great wind came across the desert, struck the four corners of the house, and it fell on the young people, and they are dead; I alone have escaped to tell you.'
²⁰Then Job arose, tore his robe, shaved his head, and fell on the ground and worshipped. ²¹He said, 'Naked I came from my mother's womb, and

naked shall I return there; the Lord gave, and the Lord has taken away; blessed be the name of the Lord.'
²²In all this Job did not sin or charge God with wrong-doing.

Narrator 2
One day the heavenly beings came to present themselves before the Lord, and Satan also came among them to present himself before the Lord. ³The Lord said to Satan, 'Have you considered my servant Job? He still persists in his integrity, although you incited me against him, to destroy him for no reason.' ⁴Then Satan answered the Lord, 'Skin for skin! All that people have they will give to save their lives. ⁵But stretch out your hand now and touch his bone and his flesh, and he will curse you to your face.' ⁶The Lord said to Satan, 'Very well, he is in your power; only spare his life.'
⁷So Satan went out from the presence of the Lord, and inflicted loathsome sores on Job from the sole of his foot to the crown of his head. ⁸Job took a potsherd with which to scrape himself, and sat among the ashes.

Narrator 1
⁹Then his wife said to him, 'Do you still persist in your integrity? Curse God, and die.' ¹⁰But he said to her, 'You speak as any foolish woman would. Shall we receive good at the hand of God, and not receive evil?' In all this Job did not sin with his lips.

¹¹Now when Job's three friends heard of all these troubles that had come upon him, each of them set out from his home – Eliphaz, Bildad, and Zophar. They met together to go and console and comfort him. ¹²When they saw him from a distance, they did not recognise him, and they raised their voices and wept aloud. ¹³They sat with him on the ground for seven days and seven nights, and no one spoke a word to him, for they saw that his suffering was very great.

Silence for 2 minutes

After this Job opened his mouth and cursed the day of his birth.

Job

3: ³ 'Let the day perish on which I was born,
and the night that said,
"A man-child is conceived."
¹¹ 'Why did I not die at birth,
come forth from the womb and expire?
¹² Why were there knees to receive me,
or breasts for me to suck?
¹³ Now I would be lying down and quiet;
I would be asleep; then I would be at rest
¹⁴ with kings and counsellors of the earth,
where slaves are free from their masters.

²⁰ 'Why is light given to one in misery,
and life to the bitter in soul,
²¹ who long for death, but it does not come,
and dig for it more than for hidden treasures.

Eliphaz

4: ² 'If one ventures a word with you, will you be offended?
But who can keep from speaking?
³ See, you have instructed many;
you have strengthened the weak hands.
⁴ Your words have supported those who were stumbling,
and you have made firm the feeble knees.
⁵ But now it has come to you, and you are impatient;
it touches you, and you are dismayed.
⁶ Is not your fear of God your confidence,
and the integrity of your ways your hope?

⁷ 'Think now, who that was innocent ever perished?
Or where were the upright cut off?
⁸ As I have seen, those who plough iniquity
and sow trouble reap the same.
⁹ By the breath of God they perish,
and by the blast of his anger they are consumed.

¹⁷ 'How happy is the one whom God reproves;
therefore do not despise the discipline of the Almighty.
¹⁸ For he wounds, but he binds up;
he strikes, but his hands heal.
¹⁹ He will deliver you from six troubles;
in seven no harm shall touch you.

²⁵ You shall know that your descendants will be many,
and your offspring like the grass of the earth.
²⁶ You shall come to your grave in ripe old age,
²⁷ See, we have searched this out; it is true.
Hear, and know it for yourself.'

Job

6: ² 'O that my vexation were weighed,
and all my calamity laid in the balances!
³ For then it would be heavier than the sand of the sea;
therefore my words have been rash.

7: ¹ 'Do not human beings have a hard service on earth,
and are not their days like the days of a labourer?
² Like a slave who longs for shade,
and like labourers who look for their wages,
³ so I am allotted months of emptiness,
and nights of misery are apportioned to me.
⁴ When I lie down I say, "When shall I rise?"
But the night is long, and I am full of tossing until dawn.
⁶ My days are swifter than a weaver's shuttle,
and come to their end without hope.
¹¹ 'Therefore I will not restrain my mouth;
I will speak in the anguish of my spirit;
I will complain in the bitterness of my soul.

²⁰ If I sin, what do I do to you, you watcher of humanity?
Why have you made me your target?
Why have I become a burden to you?
²¹ Why do you not pardon my transgression
and take away my iniquity?

For now I shall lie in the earth;
you will seek me, but I shall not be.'

Bildad

8: ² 'How long will you say these things,
and the words of your mouth be a great wind?
³ Does God pervert justice?
Or does the Almighty pervert the right?
⁴ If your children sinned against him,
he delivered them into the power of their transgression.
⁵ If you will seek God
and make supplication to the Almighty,
⁶ if you are pure and upright,
surely then he will rouse himself for you
and restore to you your rightful place.

²⁰ 'See, God will not reject a blameless person,
nor take the hand of evildoers.
²¹ He will yet fill your mouth with laughter,
and your lips with shouts of joy.
²² Those who hate you will be clothed with shame,
and the tent of the wicked will be no more.'

Job

9: ² 'Indeed I know that this is so;
but how can a mortal be just before God?
⁵ He who removes mountains, and they do not know it,
when he overturns them in his anger;
⁸ who alone stretched out the heavens
and trampled the waves of the Sea;
¹⁰ who does great things beyond understanding,
and marvellous things without number.
¹¹ Look, he passes by me, and I do not see him;
he moves on, but I do not perceive him.
¹² He snatches away; who can stop him?
Who will say to him, "What are you doing?"

¹⁴ How then can I answer him,
choosing my words with him?
¹⁵ Though I am innocent, I cannot answer him;
I must appeal for mercy to my accuser.
¹⁶ If I summoned him and he answered me,
I do not believe that he would listen to my voice.
¹⁷ For he crushes me with a tempest,
and multiplies my wounds without cause;
¹⁸ he will not let me get my breath,
but fills me with bitterness.
¹⁹ If it is a contest of strength, he is the strong one!
If it is a matter of justice, who can summon him?
²⁰ Though I am innocent,
my own mouth would condemn me;
though I am blameless, he would prove me perverse.

²² It is all one; therefore I say,
he destroys both the blameless and the wicked.
²³ When disaster brings sudden death,
he mocks at the calamity of the innocent.
²⁴ The earth is given into the hand of the wicked;
he covers the eyes of its judges–
if it is not he, who then is it?

Let me alone, that I may find a little comfort
²¹ before I go, never to return,
to the land of gloom and deep darkness,
²² the land of gloom and chaos,
where the only light is darkness.'

Zophar

11: ² 'Should a multitude of words go unanswered,
and should one full of talk be vindicated?
³ Should your babble put others to silence,
and when you mock, shall no one shame you?
⁴ For you say, "My conduct is pure,
and I am clean in God's sight."
⁵ But O that God would speak,
and open his lips to you,

⁶ and that he would tell you the secrets of wisdom!
For wisdom is many-sided.
Know then that God exacts of you
less than your guilt deserves.

¹⁴ If iniquity is in your hand, put it far away,
and do not let wickedness reside in your tents.
¹⁵ Surely then you will lift up your face without blemish;
you will be secure, and will not fear.
¹⁷ Your life will be brighter than the noonday;
its darkness will be like the morning.
²⁰ But the eyes of the wicked will fail;
all way of escape will be lost to them,
their only hope is to breathe their last.'

Job

12: ² 'No doubt you are the people,
and wisdom will die with you.
³ But I have understanding as well as you;
I am not inferior to you.

¹³ 'With God are wisdom and strength;
he has counsel and understanding.
¹⁴ If he tears down, no one can rebuild;
if he shuts a man in, no one can open up.
¹⁵ If he withholds the waters, they dry up;
if he sends them out, they overwhelm the land.

¹³ 'Look, my eye has seen all this,
my ear has heard and understood it.
² What you know, I also know;
I am not inferior to you.

³ But I would speak to the Almighty,
and I desire to argue my case with God.
⁴ As for you, you whitewash with lies;
all of you are worthless physicians.
⁵ If you would only keep silent,
that would be your wisdom!

¹² Your maxims are proverbs of ashes,
your defences are defences of clay.
¹³ 'Let me have silence, and I will speak,
and let come on me what may.

²³ How many are my iniquities and my sins?
Make me know my transgression and my sin.
²⁴ Why do you hide your face,
and count me as your enemy?
²⁶ For you write bitter things against me,
and make me reap the iniquities of my youth.

'Man, born of woman, few of days and full of trouble,
² comes up like a flower and withers,
flees like a shadow and does not last.

¹⁸ 'But the mountain falls and crumbles away,
and the rock is removed from its place;
¹⁹ the waters wear away the stones;
the torrents wash away the soil of the earth;
so you destroy the hope of mortals.
²⁰ You prevail for ever against them, and they pass away;
you change their countenance, and send them away.
²¹ Their children come to honour, and they do not know it;
they are brought low, and it goes unnoticed.
²² They feel only the pain of their own bodies,
and mourn only for themselves.'

FIRST INTERVAL

Silence for 1 or 2 minutes

Eliphaz

² 'Should the wise answer with windy knowledge,
and fill themselves with the east wind?
³ Should they argue in unprofitable talk,
or in words with which they can do no good?
⁴ You are doing away with the fear of God,
and hindering meditation before God.

⁵ For your iniquity teaches your mouth,
and you choose the tongue of the crafty.
⁶ Your own mouth condemns you, and not I;
your own lips testify against you.

¹² Why does your heart carry you away,
and why do your eyes flash,
¹³ so that you turn your spirit against God,
and let such words go out of your mouth?
¹⁴ What are mortals, that they can be clean?
Or those born of woman, that they can be righteous?
¹⁵ God puts no trust even in his holy ones,
and the heavens are not clean in his sight;
¹⁶ how much less one who is abominable and corrupt,
one who drinks iniquity like water!

¹⁷ 'I will show you; listen to me;
what I have seen I will declare—
²⁰ The wicked writhe in pain all their days,
through all the years that are laid up for the ruthless.
²⁹ They will not be rich, and their wealth will not endure,
nor will they strike root in the earth;
³⁴ For the company of the godless is barren,
and fire consumes the tents of bribery.

Job

16: ² 'I have heard many such things;
miserable comforters are you all.
⁴ I also could talk as you do,
if you were in my place;
I could join words together against you,
and shake my head at you.

⁶ 'If I speak, my pain is not assuaged,
and if I forbear, how much of it leaves me?
⁷ Surely now God has worn me out;
he has made desolate all my company.
¹² I was at ease, and he broke me in two;
he seized me by the neck and dashed me to pieces;

²⁰ My friends scorn me;
my eye pours out tears to God,
¹⁷ My spirit is broken, my days are extinct,
the grave is ready for me.
¹⁵ Where then is my hope?
Who will see my hope?
¹⁶ Will it go down to the bars of the Pit?
Shall we descend together into the dust?'

Bildad

³ Why are we counted as cattle?
Why are we stupid in your sight?
⁴ You who tear yourself in your anger—
shall the earth be forsaken because of you,
or the rock be removed out of its place?

⁵ 'Surely the light of the wicked is put out,
and the flame of their fire does not shine.
¹³ By disease their skin is consumed,
the firstborn of Death consumes their limbs.
¹⁹ They have no offspring
or descendant among their people,
and no survivor where they used to live.
²¹ Surely such are the dwellings of the ungodly,
such is the place of those who do not know God.'

Job

19: ² 'How long will you torment me,
and break me in pieces with words?
³ These ten times you have cast reproach upon me;
are you not ashamed to wrong me?
⁴ And even if it is true that I have erred,
my error remains with me.

¹¹ He has kindled his wrath against me,
and counts me as his adversary.
¹³ 'He has put my family far from me,
and my acquaintances are wholly estranged from me.

¹⁷ My breath is repulsive to my wife;
I am loathsome to my own family.
¹⁹ All my intimate friends abhor me,
and those whom I loved have turned against me.
²¹ Have pity on me, have pity on me, O you my friends,
for the hand of God has touched me!
²² Why do you, like God, pursue me,
never satisfied with my flesh?

²³ 'O that my words were written down!
O that they were inscribed in a book!
²⁴ O that with an iron pen and with lead
they were engraved on a rock for ever!
²⁵ For I know that my Redeemer lives,
and that at the last he will stand upon the earth;
²⁶ and after my skin has been thus destroyed,
then in my flesh I shall see God,
²⁷ whom I shall see on my side,
and my eyes shall behold, and not another.
My heart faints within me!

Zophar

20: ² 'Pay attention! My thoughts urge me to answer,
because of the agitation within me.
³ I hear censure that insults me,
and a spirit beyond my understanding answers me.
⁴ Do you not know this from of old,
ever since mortals were placed on earth,
⁵ that the exulting of the wicked is short,
and the joy of the godless is but for a moment?

⁶ Even though they mount up high as the heavens,
and their head reaches to the clouds,
⁷ they will perish for ever like their own dung;
those who have seen them will say, "Where are they?"
¹² 'Though wickedness is sweet in their mouth,
though they hide it under their tongues,
¹⁴ yet their food is turned in their stomachs;
it is the venom of asps within them.

¹⁹ For they have crushed and abandoned the poor,
they have seized a house that they did not build.

²⁷ The heavens will reveal their iniquity,
and the earth will rise up against them.
²⁸ The possessions of their house will be carried away,
dragged off on the day of God's wrath.
²⁹ This is the portion of the wicked from God,
the heritage decreed for them by God.'

Job

21: ² 'Listen carefully to my words,
and let this be your consolation.
³ Bear with me, and I will speak;
then after I have spoken, mock on.

⁷ Why do the wicked live on,
reach old age, and grow mighty in power?
⁸ Their children are established in their presence,
and their offspring before their eyes.
¹³ They spend their days in prosperity,
and in peace they go down to Sheol.
¹⁴ They say to God, "Leave us alone!
We do not desire to know your ways.
¹⁵ What is the Almighty, that we should serve him?
And what profit do we get if we pray to him?"

¹⁷ 'How often is the lamp of the wicked put out?
How often does calamity come upon them?
¹⁹ You say, "God stores up their iniquity for their children."
Let it be paid back to them, so that they may know it.
²⁰ Let their own eyes see their destruction,
and let them drink of the wrath of the Almighty.
²¹ For what do they care for their household after them,
when the number of their months is cut off?

²⁹ Have you not asked those who travel the roads,
and do you not accept their testimony,
³⁰ that the wicked are spared on the day of calamity,

and are rescued on the day of wrath?
³⁴ How then will you comfort me with empty nothings
There is nothing left of your answers but falsehood.'

SECOND INTERVAL

Silence for 1 or 2 minutes

Eliphaz

22: ² 'Can a mortal be of use to God?
Can even the wisest be of service to him?
³ Is it any pleasure to the Almighty if you are righteous,
or is it gain to him if you make your ways blameless?
⁴ Is it for your piety that he reproves you,
and enters into judgement with you?
⁵ Is not your wickedness great?
There is no end to your iniquities.
⁶ For you have exacted pledges from your family,
and stripped the naked of their clothing.
⁷ You have given no water to the weary to drink,
and you have withheld bread from the hungry.

²¹ 'Agree with God, and be at peace;
in this way good will come to you.
²³ If you return to the Almighty, you will be restored,
if you remove unrighteousness from your tents,
²⁶ then you will delight in the Almighty,
and lift up your face to God.
²⁷ You will pray to him, and he will hear you,
and light will shine on your ways.

Job

23: ² 'Today also my complaint is bitter;
his hand is heavy despite my groaning.
³ O that I knew where I might find him,
that I might come even to his dwelling!

⁴ I would lay my case before him,
and fill my mouth with arguments.

⁸ 'If I go forward, he is not there;
or backward, I cannot perceive him;
⁹ on the left he hides, and I cannot behold him;
I turn to the right, but I cannot see him.
¹⁰ But he knows the way that I take;
when he has tested me, I shall come out like gold.
²⁴ 'Why are times not kept by the Almighty,
and why do those who know him never see his days?
² The wicked remove landmarks;
they seize flocks and pasture them.
³ They drive away the donkey of the orphan;
they take the widow's ox for a pledge.
¹² From the city the dying groan,
and the throat of the wounded cries for help;
yet God pays no attention to their prayer.

²² For God prolongs the life of the mighty by his power;
they rise up when they despair of life.
²⁵ If it is not so, who will prove me a liar,
and show that there is nothing in what I say?'

Bildad

25: ² 'Dominion and fear belong to God;
he makes peace in his high heaven.
³ Is there any number to his armies?
Upon whom does his light not arise?
⁴ How then can a mortal be righteous before God?
How can one born of woman be pure?
⁵ If even the moon is not bright
and the stars are not pure in his sight,
⁶ how much less a mortal, who is a maggot,
and a human being, who is a worm!'

Job

26: ² 'How you have helped one who has no power!
How you have assisted the arm that has no strength!
³ How you have counselled one who has no wisdom,
and given much good advice!

27: ² 'As God lives, who has taken away my right,
and the Almighty, who has made my soul bitter,
³ as long as my breath is in me
and the spirit of God is in my nostrils,
⁴ my lips will not speak falsehood,
and my tongue will not utter deceit.
⁵ Far be it from me to say that you are right;
until I die I will not put away my integrity from me.
⁶ I hold fast my righteousness, and will not let it go;
my heart does not reproach me for any of my days.

Zophar

¹¹ I will teach you concerning the hand of God;
that which is with the Almighty I will not conceal.

¹³ 'This is the portion of the wicked with God,
and the heritage that oppressors receive from the Almighty:
¹⁴ If their children are multiplied, it is for the sword;
and their offspring have not enough to eat.
¹⁵ Those who survive them, the pestilence buries,
and their widows make no lamentation.
²⁰ Terrors overtake them like a flood;
in the night a whirlwind carries them off.
²¹ The east wind lifts them up and they are gone;
it sweeps them out of their place.

Job

29: ² 'O that I were as in the months of old,
as in the days when God watched over me;
³ when his lamp shone over my head,

and by his light I walked through darkness;
⁴ when I was in my prime,
when the friendship of God was upon my tent;
⁵ when the Almighty was still with me,
when my children were around me;
⁷ When I went out to the gate of the city,
when I took my seat in the square,
⁸ the young men saw me and withdrew,
and the aged rose up and stood;
⁹ the nobles refrained from talking,
and laid their hands on their mouths;
¹² because I delivered the poor who cried,
and the orphan who had no helper.
¹³ The blessing of the wretched came upon me,
and I caused the widow's heart to sing for joy.

¹⁶ 'But now my soul is poured out within me;
days of affliction have taken hold of me.
¹⁷ The night racks my bones,
and the pain that gnaws me takes no rest.

¹⁶ 'If I have withheld anything that the poor desired,
or have caused the eyes of the widow to fail,
¹⁷ or have eaten my meal alone,
and the orphan has not eaten from it—
¹⁹ if I have seen anyone perish for lack of clothing,
or a poor person without covering,
²² then let my shoulder blade fall from my shoulder,
and let my arm be broken from its socket.

³⁵ O that I had one to hear me!
O that I had the indictment written by my adversary!
³⁶ Surely I would bind it on me like a crown;
³⁷ I would give him an account of all my steps;
like a prince I would approach him.

THIRD INTERVAL

Silence for 1 or 2 minutes

THE BOOK OF JOB

Narrator 1

> ³⁸ Then the Lord answered Job out of the whirlwind:

The LORD

> ² 'Who is this that darkens counsel
> by words without knowledge?
> ³ Gird up your loins like a man,
> I will question you, and you shall declare to me.
>
> ⁴ 'Where were you when I laid the foundation of the earth?
> Tell me, if you have understanding.
> ⁵ Who determined its measurements—surely you know!
> Or who stretched the line upon it?
> ⁶ On what were its bases sunk, or who laid its cornerstone
> ⁷ when the morning stars sang together
> and all the heavenly beings shouted for joy?

39:
> ⁵ 'Who has let the wild ass go free?
> Who has loosed the bonds of the swift ass,
> ⁶ to which I have given the steppe for its home,
> the salt land for its dwelling-place?
> ⁷ It scorns the tumult of the city;
> it does not hear the shouts of the driver.
> ⁸ It ranges the mountains as its pasture,
> and it searches after every green thing.
>
> ²⁶ 'Is it by your wisdom that the hawk soars,
> and spreads its wings towards the south?
> ²⁷ Is it at your command that the eagle mounts up
> and makes its nest on high?
> ²⁸ It lives on the rock and makes its home
> in the fastness of the rocky crag.
> ²⁹ From there it spies the prey;
> its eyes see it from far away.
> ³⁰ Its young ones suck up blood;
> and where the slain are, there it is.'

Job

42: ² 'I know that you can do all things,
and that no purpose of yours can be thwarted.
³ You said,
"Who is this that hides counsel without knowledge?"
Therefore I have uttered what I did not understand,
things too wonderful for me, which I did not know.
⁴ You said, "Hear, and I will speak;
I will question you, and you declare to me."
⁵ I had heard of you by the hearing of the ear,
but now my eye sees you;
⁶ therefore I despise myself,
and repent in dust and ashes.'

Narrator 2

⁷After the Lord had spoken these words to Job, the Lord said to Eliphaz: 'My wrath is kindled against you and against your two friends; for you have not spoken of me what is right, as my servant Job has. ⁸Now therefore take seven bulls and seven rams, and go to my servant Job, and offer up for yourselves a burnt-offering; and my servant Job shall pray for you, for I will accept his prayer not to deal with you according to your folly; for you have not spoken of me what is right, as my servant Job has done.'

Narrator 1

So Eliphaz and Bildad and Zophar went and did what the Lord had told them; and the Lord accepted Job's prayer. And the Lord restored the fortunes of Job when he had prayed for his friends; and the Lord gave Job twice as much as he had before. ¹²The Lord blessed the latter days of Job more than his beginning; and he had fourteen thousand sheep, six thousand camels, a thousand yoke of oxen, and a thousand donkeys. ¹³He also had seven sons and three daughters. ¹⁶After this Job lived for one hundred and forty years, and saw his children, and his children's children, four generations. ¹⁷And Job died, old and full of days.

THE BOOK OF JOB

Putting on Job as a Public Performance

The book of Job is perhaps the most dramatic piece of literature from the ancient world, next to the Greek tragedies. Its power comes over just by reading some of the 42 chapters of the book in the Bible. We do not know when it was written, or where or by whom. It is unique in the Bible in having as a hero someone who was not a Hebrew. It is evidently part of a whole tradition of the ancient Near East of writings exploring the problem of suffering.

However, because it is so long and has had later material added to the original, it is hard to get a sense of the overall drama. This arrangement aims to clarify the dramatic structure of the book, and so allow us to experience its emotional power.

An important task of any arranger is to reduce the actual amount of spoken words. I have reduced the amount by about half. It is generally accepted that over the centuries, between the original writing of Job and its present day form, several chapters were added, viz. chapters 28, 32-37 and 40-41. Thereafter I have reduced the text further, taking out passages which are difficult for modern audience to understand and clarifying the emotional arguments being presented. The translation used is the New Revised Standard Version, as are all Bible quotations except where indicated.

The structure of the book is three sets of dialogues between Job and his three friends. This is made explicit by the three musical interludes which form a musical commentary on the drama. Suggestions for the music are set out overleaf.

My practice is for the actors to sit on a row of chairs facing the audience and only standing up when they speak. The narrators could speak from the pulpit or the lectern. Because the performance is entirely auditory, the types of voices used are of great importance. All the speakers in the book, apart from Job's wife, are male. I suggest that the two narrators and Bildad are spoken by women. I prefer God to be visible throughout, but removed from the rest, e.g. in the church sanctuary.

Some refreshments afterwards are a help to allow people to "come down" from the emotional impact of the work.

Musical Interludes

The performance starts with two hymns, which help the audience participate in the emotional setting of the work.

The one at the beginning is the well-known harvest hymn, "We plough the fields and scatter". This was a harvest song sung by German farmers and noted down in 1782. The chorus goes;

> *"Then thank the Lord,*
> *O thank the Lord,*
> *for all his love."*

It sets the mood of unclouded happiness and prosperity with which the book of Job begins.

At the end, the audience sing "O Love that wilt not let me go". This is a moving hymn, written in 1882 by the blind Scottish minister George Matheson in just five minutes out of an experience of "the most severe mental suffering".

> O Love that wilt not let me go,
> I rest my weary soul in thee;
> I give thee back the life I owe,
> That in thine ocean depths its flow
> May richer, fuller be...

There are three musical interludes in the body of the work, after each of the three main sets of speeches. They should reflect first desolation, then despair and then storm.

The musical interludes can be provided by recorded music, by an organ pieces or by live music, e.g. a string quartet. All music should be instrumental - no singing, because the book of Job has enough words already. An exception could be renaissance liturgical music by Gesualdo, and sung in Latin.

THE BOOK OF JOB

Here are some suggestions:

Recorded music:
Musical interlude 1   Praeludio from Otello by Verdi (6 mins)
Musical interlude 2   "Death and the Maiden" by Schubert, arr. Mahler, 1st Movement, fade after 4.30 or 6.20
Musical interlude 3   Storm - Britten's Four Sea Interludes (5 mins) or Prelude to "The Tempest" by Sibelius (8 mins)

Organ music:
Musical interlude 1   Chorale prelude BWV 622 - J S Bach (5 minutes), or Chorale prelude BWV 625 - J S Bach (4 minutes)
Musical interlude 2   Postlude - 24 pieces en style libre- Vierne (2.5 mins)
Musical interlude 3   Toccata - last of Variations on a Theme by Paganini - Thalben Ball (1 minute) - possibly add a previous variation beforehand

Live Classical Music:
e.g. from Haydn's String Quartet Op.51, the Seven Last Words of Jesus Christ
Musical interlude 1   L'Introduzione
Musical interlude 2   Sonata IV: Eli, Eli, lama sabachthani?
Musical interlude 3   Il terremoto

Instrumental Hard Rock/Heavy Metal:
e.g. Iron Maiden: the Prisoner, Stranger in a strange land, Deja-vu

The Book of Job

for Public Performance

THE BOOK OF JOB

The Beginning

The evening starts by people standing and singing "We plough the fields and scatter…"

We plough the fields, and scatter
the good seed on the land,
But it is fed and watered
by God's almighty hand;
He sends the snow in winter,
the warmth to swell the grain,
The breezes and the sunshine,
and soft refreshing rain.
All good gifts around us
Are sent from heaven above,
Then thank the Lord, O thank the Lord
For all His love.

He only is the Maker
of all things near and far;
He paints the wayside flower,
He lights the evening star;
The winds and waves obey Him,
by Him the birds are fed;
Much more to us, His children,
He gives our daily bread.

We thank Thee, then, O Father,
for all things bright and good,
The seed time and the harvest,
our life, our health, and food;
No gifts have we to offer,
for all Thy love imparts,
But that which Thou desirest,
our humble, thankful hearts.

Introduction

Narrator 1
There was once a man in the land of Uz whose name was Job. That man was blameless and upright, one who feared God and turned away from evil. ²There were born to him seven sons and three daughters. ³He had seven thousand sheep, three thousand camels, five hundred yoke of oxen, five hundred donkeys, and very many servants; so that this man was the greatest of all the people of the east. ⁴His sons used to go and hold feasts in one another's houses in turn; and they would send and invite their three sisters to eat and drink with them. ⁵And when the feast days had run their course, Job would send and sanctify them, and he would rise early in the morning and offer burnt-offerings according to the number of them all; for Job said, 'It may be that my children have sinned, and cursed God in their hearts.' This is what Job always did.

Narrator 2
⁶One day the heavenly beings came to present them-selves before the Lord, and Satan also came among them. ⁷The Lord said to Satan, 'Where have you come from?' Satan answered the Lord, 'From going to and fro on the earth, and from walking up and down on it.' ⁸The Lord said to Satan, 'Have you considered my servant Job? There is no one like him on the earth, a blameless and upright man who fears God and turns away from evil.' ⁹Then Satan answered the Lord, 'Does Job fear God for nothing? ¹⁰Have you not put a fence around him and his house and all that he has, on every side? You have blessed the work of his hands, and his possessions have increased in the land. ¹¹But stretch out your hand now, and touch all that he has, and he will curse you to your face.' ¹²The Lord said to Satan, 'Very well, all that he has is in your power; only do not stretch out your hand against him!' So Satan went out from the presence of the Lord.

Narrator 1
¹³One day when his sons and daughters were eating and drinking wine in the eldest brother's house, ¹⁴a messenger came to Job and said, 'The oxen were ploughing and the donkeys were feeding beside them, ¹⁵and the Sabeans fell on them and carried them off, and killed the servants with the edge of the sword; I alone have escaped to tell you.' ¹⁶While he was

THE BOOK OF JOB

still speaking, another came and said, 'The fire of God fell from heaven and burned up the sheep and the servants, and consumed them; I alone have escaped to tell you.' [17]While he was still speaking, another came and said, 'The Chaldeans formed three columns, made a raid on the camels and carried them off, and killed the servants with the edge of the sword; I alone have escaped to tell you.' [18]While he was still speaking, another came and said, 'Your sons and daughters were eating and drinking wine in their eldest brother's house, [19]and suddenly a great wind came across the desert, struck the four corners of the house, and it fell on the young people, and they are dead; I alone have escaped to tell you.'

[20]Then Job arose, tore his robe, shaved his head, and fell on the ground and worshipped. [21]He said, 'Naked I came from my mother's womb, and naked shall I return there; the Lord gave, and the Lord has taken away; blessed be the name of the Lord.'

[22]In all this Job did not sin or charge God with wrongdoing.

INTRODUCTION

Narrator 2

One day the heavenly beings came to present themselves before the Lord, and Satan also came among them to present himself before the Lord. ²The Lord said to Satan, 'Where have you come from?' Satan answered the Lord, 'From going to and fro on the earth, and from walking up and down on it.' ³The Lord said to Satan, 'Have you considered my servant Job? There is no one like him on the earth, a blameless and upright man who fears God and turns away from evil. He still persists in his integrity, although you incited me against him, to destroy him for no reason.' ⁴Then Satan answered the Lord, 'Skin for skin! All that people have they will give to save their lives. ⁵But stretch out your hand now and touch his bone and his flesh, and he will curse you to your face.' ⁶The Lord said to Satan, 'Very well, he is in your power; only spare his life.'

⁷So Satan went out from the presence of the Lord, and inflicted loathsome sores on Job from the sole of his foot to the crown of his head. ⁸Job took a potsherd with which to scrape himself, and sat among the ashes.

Narrator 1

⁹Then his wife said to him, 'Do you still persist in your integrity? Curse God, and die.' ¹⁰But he said to her, 'You speak as any foolish woman would. Shall we receive good at the hand of God, and not receive evil?' In all this Job did not sin with his lips.

¹¹Now when Job's three friends heard of all these trou-bles that had come upon him, each of them set out from his home - Eliphaz the Temanite, Bildad the Shuhite, and Zophar the Naamathite. They met together to go and console and comfort him. ¹²When they saw him from a distance, they did not recognise him, and they raised their voices and wept aloud; they tore their robes and threw dust in the air upon their heads. ¹³They sat with him on the ground for seven days and seven nights, and no one spoke a word to him, for they saw that his suffering was very great.

Silence for 2 minutes

After this Job opened his mouth and cursed the day of his birth.

THE BOOK OF JOB

First Cycle

Job

3: ³ 'Let the day perish on which I was born,
and the night that said,
"A man-child is conceived."
⁴ Let that day be darkness!
⁵ Let gloom and deep darkness claim it.
⁶ That night—let thick darkness seize it!
let it not rejoice among the days of the year;
⁷ Yes, let that night be barren;
let no joyful cry be heard in it.
⁹ Let the stars of its dawn be dark;
let it hope for light, but have none;
¹⁰ because it did not shut the doors of my mother's womb,
and hide trouble from my eyes.

¹¹ 'Why did I not die at birth,
come forth from the womb and expire?
¹² Why were there knees to receive me,
or breasts for me to suck?
¹³ Now I would be lying down and quiet;
I would be asleep; then I would be at rest
¹⁴ with kings and counsellors of the earth
who rebuild ruins for themselves,
¹⁵ or with princes who have gold,
who fill their houses with silver.
¹⁶ Or why was I not buried like a stillborn child,
like an infant that never sees the light?
¹⁷ There the wicked cease from troubling,
and there the weary are at rest.
¹⁸ There the prisoners are at ease together;
they do not hear the voice of the taskmaster.
¹⁹ The small and the great are there,
and the slaves are free from their masters.

²⁰ 'Why is light given to one in misery,
and life to the bitter in soul,
²¹ who long for death, but it does not come,
and dig for it more than for hidden treasures;
²² who rejoice exceedingly,
and are glad when they find the grave?
²³ Why is light given to one who cannot see the way,
whom God has fenced in?
²⁴ For my sighing comes like my bread,
and my groanings are poured out like water.

Eliphaz

4: ² 'If one ventures a word with you, will you be offended?
But who can keep from speaking?
³ See, you have instructed many;
you have strengthened the weak hands.
⁴ Your words have supported those who were stumbling,
and you have made firm the feeble knees.
⁵ But now it has come to you, and you are impatient;
it touches you, and you are dismayed.
⁶ Is not your fear of God your confidence,
and the integrity of your ways your hope?

⁷ 'Think now, who that was innocent ever perished?
Or where were the upright cut off?
⁸ As I have seen, those who plough iniquity
and sow trouble reap the same.
⁹ By the breath of God they perish,
and by the blast of his anger they are consumed.

¹² 'Now a word came stealing to me,
my ear received the whisper of it.
¹³ Amid thoughts from visions of the night,
when deep sleep falls on mortals,
¹⁴ dread came upon me, and trembling,
which made all my bones shake.
A form was before my eyes;
there was silence, then I heard a voice:

¹⁷ "Can mortals be righteous before God?
Can human beings be pure before their Maker?

¹⁸ Even in his servants he puts no trust,
and his angels he charges with error;
¹⁹ how much more those who live in houses of clay,
whose foundation is in the dust,
who are crushed like a moth.
²⁰ Between morning and evening they are destroyed;
they perish for ever without any regarding it.

5: ³ I have seen fools taking root,
but suddenly I cursed their dwelling.
⁴ Their children are far from safety,
they are crushed in the gate,
and there is no one to deliver them.
⁶ For misery does not come from the earth,
nor does trouble sprout from the ground;
⁷ but human beings are born to trouble
just as sparks fly upward.

¹⁷ 'How happy is the one whom God reproves;
therefore do not despise the discipline of the Almighty.
¹⁸ For he wounds, but he binds up;
he strikes, but his hands heal.
¹⁹ He will deliver you from six troubles;
in seven no harm shall touch you.
²⁰ In famine he will redeem you from death,
and in war from the power of the sword.

²² At destruction and famine you shall laugh,
and shall not fear the wild animals of the earth.
²⁴ You shall know that your tent is safe,
you shall inspect your fold and miss nothing.
²⁵ You shall know that your descendants will be many,
and your offspring like the grass of the earth.
²⁶ You shall come to your grave in ripe old age,
as a shock of grain comes up to the threshing-floor in its season.
²⁷ See, we have searched this out; it is true.
Hear, and know it for yourself.'

Job

6: ² 'O that my vexation were weighed,
and all my calamity laid in the balances!
³ For then it would be heavier than the sand of the sea;
therefore my words have been rash.

⁸ 'O that I might have my request,
and that God would grant my desire;
⁹ that it would please God to crush me,
that he would let loose his hand and cut me off!
¹⁰ This would be my consolation;
I would even exult in unrelenting pain;
for I have not denied the words of the Holy One.
¹¹ What is my strength, that I should wait?
And what is my end, that I should be patient?
¹² Is my strength the strength of stones,
or is my flesh bronze?
¹³ In truth I have no help in me,
and any resource is driven from me.

7: ¹ 'Do not human beings have a hard service on earth,
and are not their days like the days of a labourer?
² Like a slave who longs for the shadow,
and like labourers who look for their wages,
³ so I am allotted months of emptiness,
and nights of misery are apportioned to me.
⁴ When I lie down I say, "When shall I rise?"
But the night is long, and I am full of tossing until dawn.
⁶ My days are swifter than a weaver's shuttle,
and come to their end without hope.
¹¹ 'Therefore I will not restrain my mouth;
I will speak in the anguish of my spirit;
I will complain in the bitterness of my soul.

¹⁶ I loathe my life; I would not live for ever.
Let me alone, for my days are a breath.
¹⁷ What are human beings,
that you make so much of them,
that you set your mind on them,

[18] visit them every morning,
test them every moment?
[19] Will you not look away from me for a while,
let me alone until I swallow my spit?
[20] If I sin, what do I do to you, you watcher of humanity?
Why have you made me your target?
Why have I become a burden to you?
[21] Why do you not pardon my transgression
and take away my iniquity?
For now I shall lie in the earth;
you will seek me, but I shall not be.'

Bildad

8: [2] 'How long will you say these things,
and the words of your mouth be a great wind?
[3] Does God pervert justice?
Or does the Almighty pervert the right?
[4] If your children sinned against him,
he delivered them into the power of their transgression.
[5] If you will seek God
and make supplication to the Almighty,
[6] if you are pure and upright,
surely then he will rouse himself for you
and restore to you your rightful place.
[7] Though your beginning was small,
your latter days will be very great.

[8] 'For inquire now of bygone generations,
and consider what their ancestors have found;
[9] for we are but of yesterday, and we know nothing,
for our days on earth are but a shadow.
[10] Will they not teach you and tell you
and utter words out of their understanding?

[20] 'See, God will not reject a blameless person,
nor take the hand of evildoers.
[21] He will yet fill your mouth with laughter,
and your lips with shouts of joy.

²² Those who hate you will be clothed with shame,
and the tent of the wicked will be no more.'

Job

9: ² 'Indeed I know that this is so;
but how can a mortal be just before God?
⁴ He is wise in heart, and mighty in strength
—who has resisted him, and succeeded?—
⁵ he who removes mountains, and they do not know it,
when he overturns them in his anger;
⁸ who alone stretched out the heavens
and trampled the waves of the Sea;
⁹ who made the Bear and Orion,
the Pleiades and the chambers of the south;
¹⁰ who does great things beyond understanding,
and marvellous things without number.
¹¹ Look, he passes by me, and I do not see him;
he moves on, but I do not perceive him.
¹² He snatches away; who can stop him?
Who will say to him, "What are you doing?"

¹⁴ How then can I answer him,
choosing my words with him?
¹⁵ Though I am innocent, I cannot answer him;
I must appeal for mercy to my accuser.
¹⁶ If I summoned him and he answered me,
I do not believe that he would listen to my voice.
¹⁷ For he crushes me with a tempest,
and multiplies my wounds without cause;
¹⁸ he will not let me get my breath,
but fills me with bitterness.
¹⁹ If it is a contest of strength, he is the strong one!
If it is a matter of justice, who can summon him?
²⁰ Though I am innocent,
my own mouth would condemn me;
though I am blameless, he would prove me perverse.

'I loathe my life;
I will give free utterance to my complaint;
I will speak in the bitterness of my soul.
² I will say to God, Do not condemn me;
let me know why you contend against me.

⁸ Your hands fashioned and made me;
and now you turn and destroy me.
¹¹ You clothed me with skin and flesh,
and knit me together with bones and sinews.
¹² You have granted me life and steadfast love,
and your care has preserved my spirit.
¹³ Yet these things you hid in your heart;
I know that this was your purpose.
¹⁵ If I am wicked, woe to me!
If I am righteous, I cannot lift up my head,
¹⁶ Bold as a lion you hunt me;
and increase your vexation towards me.

¹⁸ 'Why did you bring me forth from the womb?
Would that I had died before any eye had seen me,
¹⁹ and were as though I had not been,
carried from the womb to the grave.
²⁰ Are not the days of my life few?
Let me alone, that I may find a little comfort
²¹ before I go, never to return,
to the land of gloom and deep darkness,
²² the land of gloom and chaos,
where the only light is darkness.'

Zophar

11: ² 'Should a multitude of words go unanswered,
and should one full of talk be vindicated?
³ Should your babble put others to silence,
and when you mock, shall no one shame you?
⁴ For you say, "My conduct is pure,
and I am clean in God's sight."

⁵ But O that God would speak,
and open his lips to you,
⁶ and that he would tell you the secrets of wisdom!
For wisdom is many-sided.
Know then that God exacts of you
less than your guilt deserves.

⁷ 'Can you find out the deep things of God?
Can you find out the limit of the Almighty?
⁸ It is higher than heaven—what can you do?
Deeper than Sheol—what can you know?
⁹ Its measure is longer than the earth,
and broader than the sea.
¹⁰ If he passes through, and imprisons,
and assembles for judgement, who can hinder him?
¹¹ For he knows those who are worthless;
when he sees iniquity, will he not consider it?

¹⁴ If iniquity is in your hand, put it far away,
and do not let wickedness reside in your tents.
¹⁵ Surely then you will lift up your face without blemish;
you will be secure, and will not fear.
¹⁶ You will forget your misery;
you will remember it as waters that have passed away.
¹⁷ And your life will be brighter than the noonday;
its darkness will be like the morning.
¹⁸ And you will have confidence, because there is hope;
you will be protected and take your rest in safety.
²⁰ But the eyes of the wicked will fail;
all way of escape will be lost to them,
their only hope is to breathe their last.'

Job

12:    ² 'No doubt you are the people,
and wisdom will die with you.
³ But I have understanding as well as you;
I am not inferior to you.
Who does not know such things as these?

FIRST CYCLE

¹³ 'With God are wisdom and strength;
he has counsel and understanding.
¹⁴ If he tears down, no one can rebuild;
if he shuts a man in, no one can open up.
¹⁵ If he withholds the waters, they dry up;
if he sends them out, they overwhelm the land.
²³ He makes nations great, then destroys them;
he enlarges nations, then leads them away.
²⁴ He strips understanding from the leaders of the earth,
and makes them wander in a pathless waste.
²⁵ They grope in the dark without light;
he makes them stagger like a drunken man.

13: ¹ 'Look, my eye has seen all this,
my ear has heard and understood it.
² What you know, I also know;
I am not inferior to you.

³ But I would speak to the Almighty,
and I desire to argue my case with God.
⁴ As for you, you whitewash with lies;
all of you are worthless physicians.

¹³ 'Let me have silence, and I will speak,
and let come on me what may.
¹⁴ I will take my flesh in my teeth,
and put my life in my hand.
¹⁵ See, he will kill me; I have no hope;
but I will defend my ways to his face.
¹⁸ I have indeed prepared my case;
I know that I shall be vindicated.

²³ How many are my iniquities and my sins?
Make me know my transgression and my sin.
²⁴ Why do you hide your face,
and count me as your enemy?
²⁵ Will you frighten a windblown leaf
and pursue dry chaff?
²⁶ For you write bitter things against me,
and make me reap the iniquities of my youth.

Man, born of woman, few of days and full of trouble,
² comes up like a flower and withers,
flees like a shadow and does not last.

⁷ 'There is hope for a tree,
if it is cut down, that it will sprout again,
and that its shoots will not cease.
⁸ Though its root grows old in the earth,
and its stump dies in the ground,
⁹ yet at the scent of water it will bud
and put forth branches like a young plant.
¹⁰ But mortals die, and are laid low;
humans expire, and where are they?
¹¹ As waters fail from a lake,
and a river wastes away and dries up,
¹² so mortals lie down and do not rise again;
until the heavens are no more, they will not awake
or be roused out of their sleep.

¹⁸ The mountain falls and crumbles away,
and the rock is removed from its place;
¹⁹ the waters wear away the stones;
the torrents wash away the soil of the earth;
so you destroy the hope of mortals.
²⁰ You prevail for ever against them, and they pass away;
you change their countenance, and send them away.
²¹ Their children come to honour, and they do not know it;
they are brought low, and it goes unnoticed.
²² They feel only the pain of their own bodies,
and mourn only for themselves.'

FIRST CYCLE

Musical Interlude 1

Second Cycle

Eliphaz

² 'Should the wise answer with windy knowledge,
and fill themselves with the east wind?
³ Should they argue in unprofitable talk,
or in words with which they can do no good?
⁴ But you are doing away with the fear of God,
and hindering meditation before God.
⁵ For your iniquity teaches your mouth,
and you choose the tongue of the crafty.
⁶ Your own mouth condemns you, and not I;
your own lips testify against you.

⁷ 'Are you the firstborn of the human race?
Were you brought forth before the hills?
⁸ Have you listened in the council of God?
And do you limit wisdom to yourself?
¹¹ Are the consolations of God too small for you,
or the word that deals gently with you?
¹² Why does your heart carry you away,
and why do your eyes flash,
¹³ so that you turn your spirit against God,
and let such words go out of your mouth?
¹⁴ What are mortals, that they can be clean?
Or those born of woman, that they can be righteous?
¹⁵ God puts no trust even in his holy ones,
and the heavens are not clean in his sight;
¹⁶ how much less one who is abominable and corrupt,
one who drinks iniquity like water!

¹⁷ 'I will show you; listen to me;
what I have seen I will declare -
¹⁸ what sages have told,
and their ancestors have not hidden.

²⁰ The wicked writhe in pain all their days,
through all the years that are laid up for the ruthless.
²¹ Terrifying sounds are in their ears;
in prosperity the destroyer will come upon them.
²⁵ Because they stretched out their hands against God,
and bid defiance to the Almighty,
²⁸ they will live in desolate cities,
in houses destined to become heaps of ruins;
²⁹ they will not be rich, and their wealth will not endure,
nor will they strike root in the earth;
³⁴ For the company of the godless is barren,
and fire consumes the tents of bribery.

Job

16: ² 'I have heard many such things;
miserable comforters are you all.
³ Have windy words no limit?
Or what provokes you that you keep on talking?
⁴ I also could talk as you do,
if you were in my place;
I could join words together against you,
and shake my head at you.

⁶ 'If I speak, my pain is not assuaged,
and if I forbear, how much of it leaves me?
⁷ Surely now God has worn me out;
he has made desolate all my company.
¹¹ God gives me up to the ungodly,
and casts me into the hands of the wicked.
¹² I was at ease, and he broke me in two;
he seized me by the neck and dashed me to pieces;
he set me up as his target;
¹³ his archers surround me.
He slashes open my kidneys, and shows no mercy;
he pours out my gall on the ground.
¹⁶ My face is red with weeping,
and deep darkness is on my eyelids,
¹⁷ though there is no violence in my hands,
and my prayer is pure.

18 '¹⁸ 'O earth, do not cover my blood;
let my outcry find no resting-place.
²⁰ My friends scorn me;
my eye pours out tears to God,

17:   My spirit is broken, my days are extinct,
the grave is ready for me.

⁷ My eye has grown dim from grief,
and all my members are like a shadow.
¹¹ My days are past, my plans are broken off,
even the desires of my heart.
If I spread my couch in darkness,
¹⁴ if I say to the Pit, "You are my father",
and to the worm, "My mother", or "My sister",
¹⁵ where then is my hope?
Who will see my hope?
¹⁶ Will it go down to the bars of Sheol?
Shall we descend together into the dust?'

Bildad

18:   ² 'How long will you hunt for words?
Consider, and then we shall speak.
³ Why are we counted as cattle?
Why are we stupid in your sight?
⁴ You who tear yourself in your anger -
shall the earth be forsaken because of you,
or the rock be removed out of its place?

⁵ 'Surely the light of the wicked is put out,
and the flame of their fire does not shine.
⁹ A trap seizes them by the heel;
a snare lays hold of them.
¹⁰ A rope is hid for them in the ground,
a trap for them in the path.
¹¹ Terrors frighten them on every side,
and chase them at their heels.

THE BOOK OF JOB

¹³ By disease their skin is consumed,
the firstborn of Death consumes their limbs.
¹⁴ They are torn from the tent in which they trusted,
and are brought to the king of terrors.
¹⁷ Their memory perishes from the earth,
and they have no name in the street.
¹⁸ They are thrust from light into darkness,
and driven out of the world.
¹⁹ They have no offspring
or descendant among their people,
and no survivor where they used to live.
²⁰ Those of the west are appalled at their fate,
and horror seizes those of the east.
²¹ Surely such are the dwellings of the ungodly,
such is the place of those who do not know God.'

Job

19:   ² 'How long will you torment me,
and break me in pieces with words?
³ These ten times you have cast reproach upon me;
are you not ashamed to wrong me?
⁴ And even if it is true that I have erred,
my error remains with me.
⁵ If indeed you magnify yourselves against me,
and make my humiliation an argument against me,
⁶ know then that God has put me in the wrong,
and closed his net around me.
⁷ Even when I cry out, "Violence!" I am not answered;
I call aloud, but there is no justice.
⁸ He has walled up my way so that I cannot pass,
and he has set darkness upon my paths.
⁹ He has stripped my glory from me,
and taken the crown from my head.
¹⁰ He breaks me down on every side, and I am gone,
he has uprooted my hope like a tree.

¹¹ He has kindled his wrath against me,
and counts me as his adversary.

¹² His troops come on together;
they have thrown up siege-works against me,
and encamp around my tent.

¹³ 'He has put my family far from me,
and my acquaintances are wholly estranged from me.
¹⁴ My relatives and my close friends have failed me;
¹⁵ the guests in my house have forgotten me;
my serving-girls count me as a stranger;
I have become an alien in their eyes.
¹⁷ My breath is repulsive to my wife;
I am loathsome to my own family.
¹⁹ All my intimate friends abhor me,
and those whom I loved have turned against me.
²⁰ My bones cling to my skin and to my flesh,
and I have escaped by the skin of my teeth.
²¹ Have pity on me, have pity on me, O you my friends,
for the hand of God has touched me!
²² Why do you, like God, pursue me,
never satisfied with my flesh?

²³ 'O that my words were written down!
O that they were inscribed in a book!
²⁴ O that with an iron pen and with lead
they were engraved on a rock for ever!
²⁵ For I know that my Redeemer lives,
and that at the last he will stand upon the earth;
²⁶ and after my skin has been thus destroyed,
then in my flesh I shall see God,
²⁷ whom I shall see on my side,
and my eyes shall behold, and not another.
My heart faints within me!

Zophar

20: ² 'Pay attention! My thoughts urge me to answer,
because of the agitation within me.
³ I hear censure that insults me,
and a spirit beyond my understanding answers me.
⁴ Do you not know this from of old,
ever since mortals were placed on earth,
⁵ that the exulting of the wicked is short,
and the joy of the godless is but for a moment?

⁶ Even though they mount up high as the heavens,
and their head reaches to the clouds,
⁷ they will perish for ever like their own dung;
those who have seen them will say, "Where are they?"
⁸ They will fly away like a dream, and not be found;
they will be chased away like a vision of the night.
⁹ The eye that saw them will see them no more,
nor will their place behold them any longer.
¹² 'Though wickedness is sweet in their mouth,
though they hide it under their tongues,
¹⁴ yet their food is turned in their stomachs;
it is the venom of asps within them.
¹⁵ They swallow down riches and vomit them up again;
God casts them out of their bellies.
¹⁸ They will give back the fruit of their toil,
and will not swallow it down;
from the profit of their trading
they will get no enjoyment.
¹⁹ For they have crushed and abandoned the poor,
they have seized a house that they did not build.

²⁰ 'They knew no quiet in their bellies;
in their greed they let nothing escape.
²¹ There was nothing left after they had eaten;
therefore their prosperity will not endure.
²³ To fill their belly to the full
God will send his fierce anger into them,
and rain it upon them as their food.

²⁷ The heavens will reveal their iniquity,
and the earth will rise up against them.
²⁸ The possessions of their house will be carried away,
dragged off on the day of God's wrath.
²⁹ This is the portion of the wicked from God,
the heritage decreed for them by God.'

Job

21: ² 'Listen carefully to my words,
and let this be your consolation.
³ Bear with me, and I will speak;
then after I have spoken, mock on.

⁷ Why do the wicked live on,
reach old age, and grow mighty in power?
⁸ Their children are established in their presence,
and their offspring before their eyes.
⁹ Their houses are safe from fear,
and no rod of God is upon them.
¹⁰ Their bull breeds without fail;
their cow calves and never miscarries.
¹¹ They send out their little ones like a flock,
and their children dance around.
¹² They sing to the tambourine and the lyre,
and rejoice to the sound of the pipe.
¹³ They spend their days in prosperity,
and in peace they go down to Sheol.
¹⁴ They say to God, "Leave us alone!
We do not desire to know your ways.
¹⁵ What is the Almighty, that we should serve him?
And what profit do we get if we pray to him?"

¹⁷ 'How often is the lamp of the wicked put out?
How often does calamity come upon them?
¹⁹ You say, "God stores up their iniquity for their children."
Let it be paid back to them, so that they may know it.
²⁰ Let their own eyes see their destruction,
and let them drink of the wrath of the Almighty.

²¹ For what do they care for their household after them,
when the number of their months is cut off?
²³ One dies in full prosperity,
being wholly at ease and secure,
²⁴ his loins full of milk
and the marrow of his bones moist.
²⁵ Another dies in bitterness of soul,
never having tasted of good.
²⁶ They lie down alike in the dust,
and the worms cover them.

²⁷ 'Oh, I know your thoughts,
and your schemes to wrong me.
²⁸ For you say, "Where is the house of the prince?
Where is the tent in which the wicked lived?"
²⁹ Have you not asked those who travel the roads,
and do you not accept their testimony,
³⁰ that the wicked are spared on the day of calamity,
and are rescued on the day of wrath?
³⁴ How then will you comfort me with empty nothings
There is nothing left of your answers but falsehood.'

SECOND CYCLE

Musical Interlude 2

Third Cycle

Eliphaz

22: ² 'Can a mortal be of use to God?
Can even the wisest be of service to him?
³ Is it any pleasure to the Almighty if you are righteous,
or is it gain to him if you make your ways blameless?
⁴ Is it for your piety that he reproves you,
and enters into judgement with you?
⁵ Is not your wickedness great?
There is no end to your iniquities.
⁶ For you have exacted pledges from your family,
and stripped the naked of their clothing.
⁷ You have given no water to the weary to drink,
and you have withheld bread from the hungry.
⁹ You have sent widows away empty-handed,
and the arms of the orphans you have crushed.
¹⁰ Therefore snares are around you,
and sudden terror overwhelms you.

¹² 'Is not God high in the heavens?
See the highest stars, how lofty they are!
¹³ Therefore you say, "What does God know?
Can he judge through the deep darkness?
¹⁴ Thick clouds enwrap him, so that he does not see,
and he walks on the dome of heaven."
¹⁵ Will you keep to the old way
that the wicked have trod?
¹⁷ They said to God, "Leave us alone",
and "What can the Almighty do to us?"
¹⁸ Yet he filled their houses with good things -
but the plans of the wicked are repugnant to me.
¹⁹ The righteous see it and are glad;
the innocent laugh them to scorn,
²⁰ saying, "Surely our adversaries are cut off,

and what they left, the fire has consumed."
²¹ 'Agree with God, and be at peace;
 in this way good will come to you.
²² Receive instruction from his mouth,
and lay up his words in your heart.
²³ If you return to the Almighty, you will be restored,
if you remove unrighteousness from your tents,
²⁵ and if the Almighty is your gold
and your precious silver,
²⁶ then you will delight in the Almighty,
and lift up your face to God.
²⁷ You will pray to him, and he will hear you,
and light will shine on your ways.

Job

23:    ² 'Today also my complaint is bitter;
his hand is heavy despite my groaning.
³ O that I knew where I might find him,
that I might come even to his dwelling!
⁴ I would lay my case before him,
and fill my mouth with arguments.
⁵ I would learn what he would answer me,
and understand what he would say to me.
⁶ Would he contend with me in the greatness of his power?
No; but he would give heed to me.
⁷ There an upright person could reason with him,
and I should be acquitted for ever by my judge.

⁸ 'If I go forward, he is not there;
or backward, I cannot perceive him;
⁹ on the left he hides, and I cannot behold him;
I turn to the right, but I cannot see him.
¹⁰ But he knows the way that I take;
when he has tested me, I shall come out like gold.
¹¹ My foot has held fast to his steps;
I have kept his way and have not turned aside.
¹² I have not departed from the commandment of his lips;
I have treasured in my bosom the words of his mouth.

¹³ But he stands alone and who can dissuade him?
What he desires, that he does.

24: 'Why are times not kept by the Almighty,
and why do those who know him never see his days?
² The wicked remove landmarks;
they seize flocks and pasture them.
³ They drive away the donkey of the orphan;
they take the widow's ox for a pledge.
⁴ They thrust the needy off the road;
the poor of the earth all hide themselves.
⁶ They reap in a field not their own
and they glean in the vineyard of the wicked.
⁷ They lie all night naked, without clothing,
and have no covering in the cold.
⁸ They are wet with the rain of the mountains,
and cling to the rock for want of shelter.
¹² From the city the dying groan,
and the throat of the wounded cries for help;
yet God pays no attention to their prayer.

¹³ 'There are those who rebel against the light,
who are not acquainted with its ways,
and do not stay in its paths.
¹⁴ The murderer rises at dusk
to kill the poor and needy,
and in the night is like a thief.
¹⁵ The eye of the adulterer also waits for the twilight,
saying, "No eye will see me";
and he disguises his face.
¹⁶ In the dark they dig through houses;
by day they shut themselves up;
they do not know the light.
¹⁷ For deep darkness is morning to all of them;
for they are friends with the terrors of deep darkness.

²² Yet God prolongs the life of the mighty by his power;
they rise up when they despair of life.
²⁵ If it is not so, who will prove me a liar,
and show that there is nothing in what I say?'

Bildad

25: ² 'Dominion and fear belong to God;
he makes peace in his high heaven.
³ Is there any number to his armies?
Upon whom does his light not arise?
⁴ How then can a mortal be righteous before God?
How can one born of woman be pure?
⁵ If even the moon is not bright
and the stars are not pure in his sight,
⁶ how much less a mortal, who is a maggot,
and a human being, who is a worm!'

Job

26: ² 'How you have helped one who has no power!
How you have assisted the arm that has no strength!
³ How you have counselled one who has no wisdom,
and given much good advice!
⁴ With whose help have you uttered words,
and whose spirit has come forth from you?
⁵ The shades below tremble,
the waters and their inhabitants.
¹⁰ He has described a circle on the face of the waters,
at the boundary between light and darkness.
¹¹ The pillars of heaven tremble,
and are astounded at his rebuke.
¹² By his power he stilled the Sea;
by his understanding he struck down Egypt.
¹⁴ These are indeed but the outskirts of his ways;
and how small a whisper do we hear of him!
But the thunder of his power who can understand?'

27: ² 'As God lives, who has taken away my right,
and the Almighty, who has made my soul bitter,
³ as long as my breath is in me
and the spirit of God is in my nostrils,
⁴ my lips will not speak falsehood,
and my tongue will not utter deceit.

⁵ Far be it from me to say that you are right;
until I die I will not put away my integrity from me.
⁶ I hold fast my righteousness, and will not let it go;
my heart does not reproach me for any of my days.

Zophar

⁷ 'May my enemy be like the wicked,
and may my opponent be like the unrighteous.
⁸ For what is the hope of the godless
when God cuts them off,
when God takes away their lives?
⁹ Will God hear their cry
when trouble comes upon them?
¹⁰ Will they take delight in the Almighty?
Will they call upon God at all times?
¹¹ I will teach you concerning the hand of God;
that which is with the Almighty I will not conceal.
¹² All of you have seen it yourselves;
why then have you become altogether vain?

¹³ 'This is the portion of the wicked with God,
and the heritage that oppressors receive from the Almighty:
¹⁴ If their children are multiplied, it is for the sword;
and their offspring have not enough to eat.
¹⁵ Those who survive them the pestilence buries,
and their widows make no lamentation.
¹⁶ Though they heap up silver like dust,
and pile up clothing like clay -
¹⁷ they may pile it up, but the just will wear it,
and the innocent will divide the silver.
²⁰ Terrors overtake them like a flood;
in the night a whirlwind carries them off.
²¹ The east wind lifts them up and they are gone;
it sweeps them out of their place.

Job

29: ² 'O that I were as in the months of old,
as in the days when God watched over me;
³ when his lamp shone over my head,
and by his light I walked through darkness;
⁴ when I was in my prime,
when the friendship of God was upon my tent;
⁵ when the Almighty was still with me,
when my children were around me;
⁷ When I went out to the gate of the city,
when I took my seat in the square,
⁸ the young men saw me and withdrew,
and the aged rose up and stood;
⁹ the nobles refrained from talking,
and laid their hands on their mouths;
¹¹ When the ear heard, it commended me,
and when the eye saw, it approved;
¹² because I delivered the poor who cried,
and the orphan who had no helper.
¹³ The blessing of the wretched came upon me,
and I caused the widow's heart to sing for joy.
¹⁵ I was eyes to the blind,
and feet to the lame.
¹⁶ I was a father to the needy,
and I championed the cause of the stranger.
²¹ 'They listened to me, and waited,
and kept silence for my counsel.
²² After I spoke they did not speak again,
and my word dropped upon them like dew.

30 'But now they make sport of me,
those who are younger than I,
whose fathers I would have disdained
to set with the dogs of my flock.
⁹ 'Now they mock me in song;
I am a byword to them.

¹⁶ 'And now my soul is poured out within me;
days of affliction have taken hold of me.

¹⁷ The night racks my bones,
and the pain that gnaws me takes no rest.
¹⁹ He has cast me into the mire,
and I have become like dust and ashes.

²⁵ Did I not weep for those whose day was hard?
Was not my soul grieved for the poor?
²⁶ But when I looked for good, evil came;
and when I waited for light, darkness came.

31:    ⁵ 'If I have walked with falsehood,
and my foot has hurried to deceit—
⁶ let me be weighed in a just balance,
and let God know my integrity!—
⁷ if my step has turned aside from the way,
and my heart has followed my eyes,
⁸ then let me sow, and another eat;
and let what grows for me be rooted out.

⁹ 'If my heart has been enticed by a woman,
and I have lain in wait at my neighbour's door;
¹⁰ then let my wife grind for another,
and let other men kneel over her.
¹¹ For that would be a heinous crime;
and it would burn to the root all my harvest.

¹⁶ 'If I have withheld anything that the poor desired,
or have caused the eyes of the widow to fail,
¹⁷ or have eaten my meal alone,
and the orphan has not eaten from it—
¹⁹ if I have seen anyone perish for lack of clothing,
or a poor person without covering,
²² then let my shoulder blade fall from my shoulder,
and let my arm be broken from its socket.

²⁴ 'If I have made gold my trust,
or called fine gold my confidence;
²⁵ if I have rejoiced because my wealth was great,
or because my hand had acquired much;

²⁶ if I have looked at the sun when it shone,
or the moon moving in splendour,
²⁷ and my heart has been secretly enticed,
and my mouth has kissed my hand;
²⁸ this also would be iniquity to be punished by the judges,
for I should have been false to God above.

³⁵ O that I had one to hear me!
O that I had the indictment written by my adversary!
³⁶ Surely I would carry it on my shoulder;
I would bind it on me like a crown;
³⁷ I would give him an account of all my steps;
like a prince I would approach him.

THIRD CYCLE

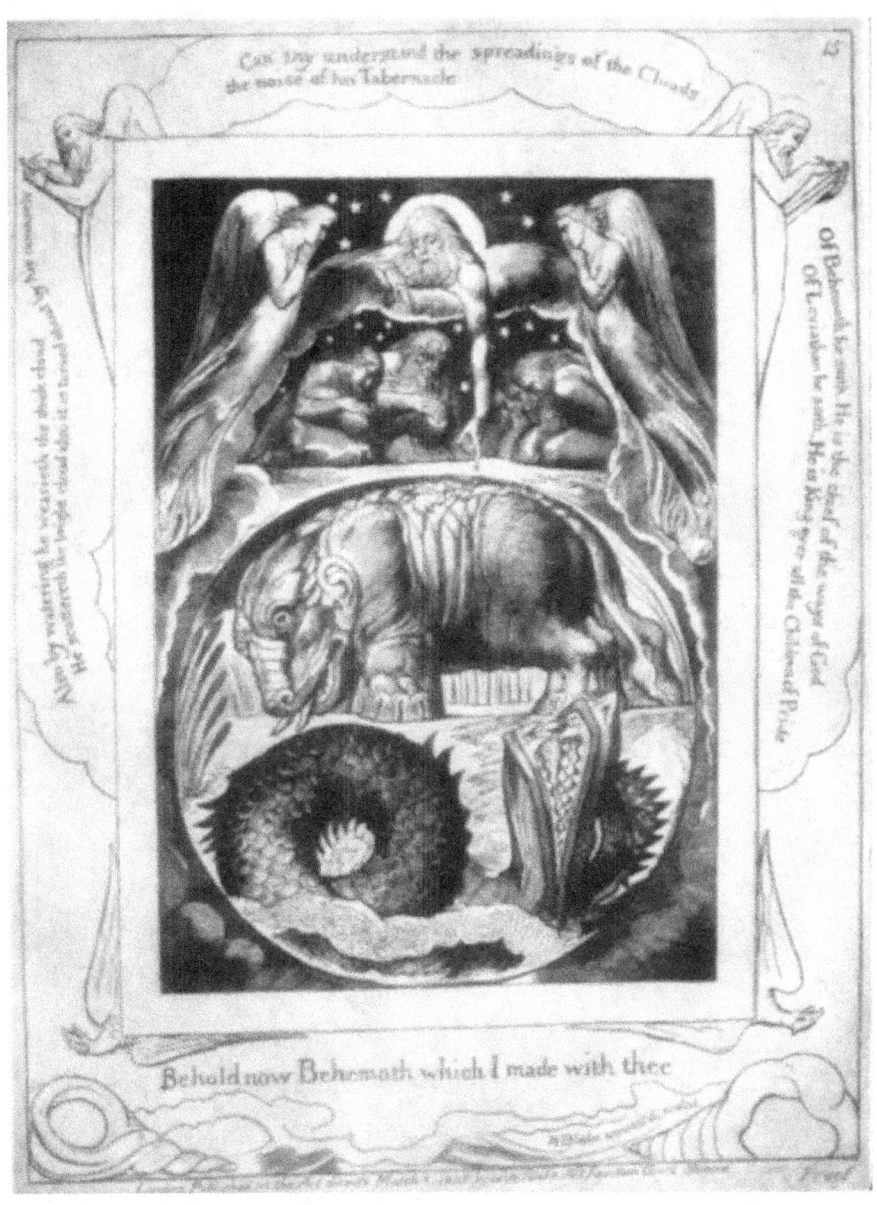

THE BOOK OF JOB

Musical Interlude 3

God Speaks

Narrator 1

38: Then the Lord answered Job out of the whirlwind:

The LORD

> [2] 'Who is this that darkens counsel
> by words without knowledge?
> [3] Gird up your loins like a man,
> I will question you, and you shall declare to me.
>
> [4] 'Where were you when I laid the foundation of the earth?
> Tell me, if you have understanding.
> [5] Who determined its measurements—surely you know!
> Or who stretched the line upon it?

⁶ On what were its bases sunk, or who laid its cornerstone
⁷ when the morning stars sang together
and all the heavenly beings shouted for joy?

⁸ 'Or who shut in the sea with doors
when it burst out from the womb?—
⁹ when I made the clouds its garment,
and thick darkness its swaddling band,
¹⁰ and prescribed bounds for it, and set bars and doors,
¹¹ and said, "Thus far shall you come, and no farther,
and here shall your proud waves be stopped"?

¹⁹ 'Where is the way to the dwelling of light,
and where is the place of darkness,
²⁰ that you may take it to its territory
and that you may discern the paths to its home?
²¹ Surely you know, for you were born then,
and the number of your days is great!

²⁵ 'Who has cut a channel for the torrents of rain,
and a way for the thunderbolt,
²⁶ to bring rain on a land where no one lives,
on the desert, which is empty of human life,
²⁷ to satisfy the waste and desolate land,
and to make the ground put forth grass?
³⁹ 'Can you hunt the prey for the lion,
or satisfy the appetite of the young lions,
⁴⁰ when they crouch in their dens,
or lie in wait in their covert?
⁴¹ Who provides for the raven its prey,
when its young ones cry to God,
and wander about for lack of food?

39:   ⁵ 'Who has let the wild ass go free?
Who has loosed the bonds of the swift ass,
⁶ to which I have given the steppe for its home,
the salt land for its dwelling-place?
⁷ It scorns the tumult of the city;
it does not hear the shouts of the driver.
⁸ It ranges the mountains as its pasture,
and it searches after every green thing.

⁹ 'Is the wild ox willing to serve you?
Will it spend the night at your crib?
¹⁰ Can you tie it in the furrow with ropes,
or will it harrow the valleys after you?
¹¹ Will you depend on it because its strength is great,
and will you hand over your labour to it?
¹² Do you have faith in it that it will return,
and bring your grain to your threshing-floor?

²⁶ 'Is it by your wisdom that the hawk soars,
and spreads its wings towards the south?
²⁷ Is it at your command that the eagle mounts up
and makes its nest on high?
²⁸ It lives on the rock and makes its home
in the fastness of the rocky crag.
²⁹ From there it spies the prey;
its eyes see it from far away.
³⁰ Its young ones suck up blood;
and where the slain are, there it is.'

THE BOOK OF JOB

The Ending

Job

42: ² 'I know that you can do all things,
    and that no purpose of yours can be thwarted.
    ³ You said,
    "Who is this that hides counsel without knowledge?"
    Therefore I have uttered what I did not understand,
    things too wonderful for me, which I did not know.
    ⁴ You said, "Hear, and I will speak;
    I will question you, and you declare to me."
    ⁵ I had heard of you by the hearing of the ear,
    but now my eye sees you;
    ⁶ therefore I despise myself,
    and repent in dust and ashes.'

Narrator 2

⁷After the Lord had spoken these words to Job, the Lord said to Eliphaz the Temanite: 'My wrath is kindled against you and against your two friends; for you have not spoken of me what is right, as my servant Job has. ⁸Now therefore take seven bulls and seven rams, and go to my servant Job, and offer up for yourselves a burnt-offering; and my servant Job shall pray for you, for I will accept his prayer not to deal with you according to your folly; for you have not spoken of me what is right, as my servant Job has done.'

Narrator 1

So Eliphaz the Temanite and Bildad the Shuhite and Zo-phar the Naamathite went and did what the Lord had told them; and the Lord accepted Job's prayer. ¹⁰And the Lord restored the fortunes of Job when he had prayed for his friends; and the Lord gave Job twice as much as he had before. ¹¹Then there came to him all his brothers and sisters and all who had known him before, and they ate bread with him in his house; they showed him sympathy and comforted him for all the evil that the Lord had

THE BOOK OF JOB

brought upon him; and each of them gave him a piece of money and a gold ring. ¹²The Lord blessed the latter days of Job more than his beginning; and he had fourteen thousand sheep, six thousand camels, a thousand yoke of oxen, and a thousand donkeys. ¹³He also had seven sons and three daughters. ¹⁴He named the first Jemimah, the second Keziah, and the third Kerenhappuch. ¹⁵In all the land there were no women so beautiful as Job's daughters; and their father gave them an inheritance along with their brothers. ¹⁶After this Job lived for one hundred and forty years, and saw his children, and his children's children, four generations. ¹⁷And Job died, old and full of days.

The Conclusion

The evening ends by people standing and singing "O Love that wilt not let me go…"

    O Love that wilt not let me go,
    I rest my weary soul in thee;
    I give thee back the life I owe,
    That in thine ocean depths its flow
    May richer, fuller be.

    O Light that followest all my way,
    I yield my flickering torch to thee;
    My heart restores its borrowed ray,
    That in thy sunshine's blaze its day
    May brighter, fairer be.

    O Joy that seekest me through pain,
    I cannot close my heart to thee;
    I trace the rainbow through the rain,
    And feel the promise is not vain,
    That morn shall tearless be.

    O Cross that liftest up my head,
    I dare not ask to fly from thee;
    I lay in dust life's glory dead,
    And from the ground there blossoms red
    Life that shall endless be.

AFTERWORD

The Meaning of Job

Lisbon

In 1755 All Saints Day, a major church festival, fell on a Saturday. It was a beautiful sunny autumn morning. Lisbon, a very religious city of about 200,000, had all the churches full for the second mass of the day when about 9.40 all the bells of the city started ringing simultaneously. A rumbling was heard leading to a series of massive bangs. The churches collapsed on the heads of the worshippers as did most of the buildings in the centre of Lisbon. People rushed terrified to the open space about the harbour and were amazed to see that the sea had vanished and the harbour was completely dry. At 10.10 a tsunami, 12 metres high, destroyed the harbour and swept thousands to their death. A terrible fire then broke out and raged for five days. At the end three quarters of the city lay in ruins and an estimated 30,000 to 60,000 had perished.

The catastrophe profoundly changed European thought. The popular understanding up till then had been that of the mathematician, scientist and Christian philosopher Gottfried Leibnitz (1646-1716), who asserted that "all was for the best in the best of all possible worlds". That optimistic view died that day. The famous French philosopher and novelist Voltaire wrote in a poem the year of the earthquake:

> "Are you then sure, the power which would create
> The universe and fix the laws of fate,
> Could not have found for man a proper place,
> But earthquakes must destroy the human race?"

His novel "Candide" is a sustained exercise of ridiculing Leibnitz's dictum. The hero, Candide, meets with disaster after disaster; after he and his companions have survived each one, Dr. Pangloss says, "You see, all these events are links in the best of all possible worlds." Candide merely replies, "That's well said, but *il faut cultiver notre jardin* - we need to cultivate our garden."

Leibnitz did not say that bad things did not happen, but that it was the overall good that counted. For Leibnitz that meant the fewest number of general laws, e.g. the laws of thermodynamics and general relativity, leading to the greatest variety of outcomes. Suffering of sentient beings was not included in Leibnitz's axiom that this was the best of all possible worlds; they were inevitable in a physical world. For instance, if we want a world with a balance of land and ocean, we need continents, which would naturally move on tectonic plates, and therefore would produce earthquakes. There is a further argument that suffering can produce new good. In Lisbon the king and the chief minister worked out the first crisis management programme; a leading aristocrat was asked "What are you going to do now?" He replied, *"Bury the dead, feed the living and close the ports."* Lisbon was rebuilt, the science of seismology was created and new earthquake-resistant houses were developed.

But none of this changed a fundamental shift in European thinking. No longer were great events seen as acts of God, sent to punish or warn or rescue. Instead they were by and large now seen as natural phenomena, independent of any divine intervention.

Trocmé

In 1934 a young Protestant pastor, Andre Trocmé, came with his family to lead a small mountain community of 3,000 at Le Chambon on the Massif Centrale. He started a private school to revive their hopes, and when war came, followed by defeat, the Vichy government and the Nazi takeover, Le Chambon became a centre of non-violent resistance. Led by their pastor, hundreds of political and Jewish refugees were saved, and the village itself was preserved from the Nazi determination to massacre civilians before the war ended. Some still fell victim to the Nazi death machine, like the splendid young man Le Forestier. Trocmé still had an absolute faith in God's ability to guide and protect those who followed him. But in July 1944, his eldest son Jean-Pierre was with an 18 year old friend Minou, and in play fired an empty revolver at her. But it had one bullet in it and the girl was killed. A month later, Jean-Pierre hanged himself. More than thirty years later, Trocmé wrote, *"There bleeds in the very depths of my being an incurable wound: an awareness of nothingness, a total resignation before nothingness, nothingness towards which I am going, and to which all those around me are going too."* (Lest Innocent Blood be Shed p. 258)

Pain

And then there's pain. Some have said that pain and suffering exist because this world is meant to be "a vale of soul-making". That sometimes happens. Some people are transformed. But not all by any means. Life in the Western world has become vastly more comfortable and secure, and so has the belief that it should always be so, that we should always be in control of events that shape our lives. It is true that a holiday camp is less likely to provide "training in righteousness" than a struggle with difficulties. But chronic pain is just as likely to unmake a soul, leading to despair. It is rather a blunt instrument for determining who is going to make it and who isn't. Philip Yancey took part in a "Make Today Count" support group of 30 terminally ill people, most in their 30s; none of their marriages remained intact over a two year period - fear and distress and guilt felt by their partners had become unbearable.

In his book, "Where is God when it Hurts?", Philip Yancey writes of a doctor, Paul Brand, who worked with leprosy patients, and of the vital importance of pain as a way the body defends itself from injury. But C. S. Lewis, in "A Grief Observed" commented, *"What is grief compared with physical pain? Whatever fools may say, the body can suffer twenty times more than the mind. The mind has always some power of evasion. At worst, the unbearable thought only comes back and back, but the physical pain can be absolutely continuous. Grief is like a bomber circling round and dropping its bombs each time the circle brings it overhead; physical pain is like the steady barrage on a trench in World War One, hours of it with no let-up for a second."* (A Grief Observed p.35)

Job

The first two chapters of the book of Job relates a series of disasters that befall Job - death and destruction caused by human wickedness; devastation of natural disasters, and finally a physical skin disease causing permanent pain and social ostracism. He has in a short space of time experienced all the worst that life can throw at us. The next 39 chapters are an impassioned debate on the meaning of life in these circumstances. But rather than an exploration of the problem of suffering, I believe they are an exploration of the problem of God.

The Problem of Suffering

People did, and do, ask "Why me?' "Why did this happen?" "Why do bad things happen to good people?" These are questions as widespread as the human race, and as old as history. But the writers of the Bible did not address these questions, just as Jesus did not.

At that very time there were some present who told Jesus about the Galileans whose blood Pilate had mingled with their sacrifices. He asked them, "Do you think that because these Galileans suffered in this way they were worse sinners than all other Galileans? No, I tell you; but unless you repent, you will all perish as they did. Or those eighteen who were killed when the tower of Siloam fell on them - do you think that they were worse offenders than all the others living in Jerusalem? No, I tell you; but unless you repent, you will all perish just as they did." (Luke 13:1-5)

The easiest way to explain suffering is that the people deserved it. It is the argument of Job's friends:

> 5 'Surely the light of the wicked is put out,
> and the flame of their fire does not shine...
> 13 By disease their skin is consumed,
> the firstborn of Death consumes their limbs.
> 14 They are torn from the tent in which they trusted,
> and are brought to the king of terrors...
> 19 They have no offspring
> or descendant among their people,
> and no survivor where they used to live...
> 21 Surely such are the dwellings of the ungodly,
> such is the place of those who do not know God.'
> (Job 18:5-21, ed.)

However, both Job - and Jesus - will have none of it.

As Jesus walked along, he saw a man blind from birth. His disciples asked him, "Rabbi, who sinned, this man or his parents, that he was born blind?" Jesus answered, "Neither this man nor his parents sinned; he was born blind so that God's works might be revealed in him." (John 9:1-2)

The danger of taking suffering as the problem, is that all too easily the sufferer can be turned into the scapegoat. "Who sinned, this man or his *parents, that he was born blind?"* It is similar to the danger of certain churches who believe in healing by faith; the sick person who is not healed may be told that it was their own lack of faith which made the prayers fail. That is spiritual abuse. We also see it today in the generally negative attitude to refugees, especially towards those fleeing from war zones where they have lost everything.

Above all, making suffering the problem drives people inevitably to some sort of intellectual solution, and intellectual solutions don't help.

The Problem of God

There are two issues which arise when we think about suffering and evil in relation to God:
1 Is God, in any useful sense of the word, real? and
2 Is God, in any useful sense of the word, good?

Is God, in any useful sense of the word, real?

There were certainly some in Israel who denied the reality of God:

> *The fool says in his heart, "There is no God".*
> *They are corrupt, their deeds are vile,*
> *there is no one who does good."*
> (Psalm 14:1 NIV)

> *I was envious of the arrogant;*
> *I saw the prosperity of the wicked…*
> *Therefore the people turn and praise them,*
> *and find no fault with them.*
> *And they say, 'How can God know?*
> *Is there knowledge in the Most High?'*
> (Psalm 73:3, 10,11)

THE BOOK OF JOB

This was seen as a moral failure rather than an intellectual or theological failure.

> *Truly, the fear of the LORD, that is wisdom,*
> *and to depart from evil is understanding.*
> (Job 28:28)

To most Israelites the reality of God was seen in the natural world around them. Bill Wilson, co-founder of Alcoholics Anonymous, gave a man-in-the-street view of God:

Despite contrary indications, I had little doubt that a mighty purpose and rhythm underlay all. How could there be so much of precise and immutable law, and no intelligence? I simply had to believe in a Spirit of the Universe, who knew neither time nor limitation. But that was as far as I had gone.
(Alcoholics Anonymous, 4th ed. p.10)

The reality of God was also seen in the historical events which led the Hebrews from slavery in Egypt to possession of the land of Canaan. But there was a problem, set out, for example, in Psalm 89. The first half recounts all the promises made to King David:

> *I have found my servant David;*
> *with my holy oil I have anointed him…*
> *I will establish his line for ever*
> *and his throne as long as the heavens endure…*

followed by a catalogue of constant and permanent promises. But verses 38 - 51 tell a different story;

> *But now you have spurned and rejected him;*
> *you are full of wrath agains your anointed…*
> *Lord, where is your steadfast love of old,*
> *which by your faithfulness you swore to David?*
> *Remember, O Lord, how your servant is taunted;*
> *how I bear in my bosom the insults of the peoples…*
> (Psalm 89: 20, 36, 38, 49, 50)

AFTERWORD

Even the most pessimistic book of the Bible, Ecclesiastes, does not doubt the reality of God. *I saw all the deeds that are done under the sun; and see, all is vanity and a chasing after wind... There is nothing better for mortals than to eat and drink, and find enjoyment in their toil. This also, I saw, is from the hand of God."* (Ecclesiastes 1.14, 2.24)

The fundamental faith statement of Judaism, the Shema'a, proclaims:

> *Hear, O Israel, the LORD our God, the LORD is one.*
> (Deuteronomy 6:4, foot-note)

Which means among other things, as I heard one rabbi expound it, he is not none.

Is God, in any useful sense of the word, good?

To proclaim, *Hear, O Israel, the LORD our God, the LORD is one*, also means that God is not many. The universe is not supported or undermined by a galaxy of co-operating, competing and warring gods. That would be one way to consign the problem of suffering into a completely different dimension, with no useful results at all.

He is not three; Christians can all too readily fall into that trap, especially in thinking that God in the New Testament is a God of love, and in the Old Testament he is a God of anger. In the Hebrew scriptures God is full of loving kindness and faithfulness. In the New Testament there are real consequences to rebelling against God. A neat distinction between Old and New Testaments simply does not exist. The faith of the Old Testament is the soil in which the Gospel grows.

And he is not two. This is the crux of the issue. It differentiates the Abrahamic faiths, Judaism, Christianity and Islam, from Zoroastrianism. This was the religion of the Persian empire from 600 BCE to 600 CE, and 2.6 million people still practice it in Iran and India. it teaches that the world is ruled by two equal and opposite deities, Ahura Mazda, the God of Wisdom, who creates and sustains the universe, and Angra Mainyu, or Angry Spirit, who was opposed in everything to the God of Wisdom. However, for no clear reason, mankind is required to follow the Creator God of Wisdom.

THE BOOK OF JOB

By asserting that God is One, both good and evil are within God's rule.

> *I form light and create darkness,*
> *I make weal and create woe;*
> *I, the LORD, do all these things.*
> (Isaiah 45.9)

If this is so, if God is master of both good and evil, how are we to maintain that God is "good"? The whole debate of the Book of Job centres round this question:

> *It is all one; therefore I say,*
> *he destroys both the blameless and the wicked.*
> *When disaster brings sudden death,*
> *he mocks at the calamity of the innocent.*
> *The earth is given into the hand of the wicked;*
> *he covers the eyes of its judges -*
> *if it is not he, who then is it?*
> (Job 9.22-24)

It is a troubling view of God, but one echoed in the prophets, notably Jeremiah:

> *Why does the way of the guilty prosper?*
> *Why do all who are treacherous thrive?*
> *You plant them, and they take root;*
> *they grow and bring forth fruit.*
> (Jeremiah 12.1-2)

> *Truly, you are to me a deceitful brook,*
> *like waters that fail.*
> (Jeremiah 15.18)

The earliest of the writing prophets, Amos, c. 750 BCE, said

> *Alas for you who desire the day of the Lord!*
> *Why do you want the day of the Lord?*
> *It is darkness, not light;*
> *as if someone fled from a lion,*
> *and was met by a bear;*

> *or went into the house and rested a hand against the wall,*
> *and was bitten by a snake.*
> *Is not the day of the Lord darkness, not light,*
> *and gloom with no brightness in it?*
> *(Amos 5.18-20)*

Psalms of lament are by far the most common type of psalm. They usually end with some expression of hope, all except Psalm 88:

> *O Lord, why do you cast me off?*
> *Why do you hide your face from me?*
> *Wretched and close to death for my youth up,*
> *I suffer your terrors; I am desperate.*
> *Your wrath has swept over me;*
> *your dread assaults destroy me.*
> *They surround me like a flood all day long;*
> *from all sides they close in on me.*
> *You have caused friend and neighbour to shun me;*
> *my companions are in darkness.*
> *(Psalm 88.14-18)*

The most powerful account of the struggle to believe that God is good comes in C. S. Lewis' book "A Grief Observed". C. S. Lewis was the most popular and powerful apologist for the Christian faith in the 20th century. But after his wife died of cancer, he found himself questioning everything. "A Grief Observed" consists of the jottings he made in four old notebooks after his wife's death as his way of coping with grief.

Sooner or later I must face the question in plain language. What reason have we, except our own desperate wishes, to believe that God is, by any standard that we can conceive, 'good'? Doesn't all the prima facie evidence suggest exactly the opposite? What have we to set against it?

We set Christ against it. But what if He were mistaken? Almost His last words may have a perfectly clear meaning. (My God, my God, why have you forsaken me?) He had found that the Being He called Father was horribly and infinitely different from what He had supposed. The trap, so long and carefully prepared and so subtly baited was at last sprung on the cross. The vile practical joke had succeeded.

THE BOOK OF JOB

Someone once said, I believe, "God always geometrizes".
Supposing the truth were, "God always vivisects?"

The next morning, he tried thinking it out again:

I wrote that last night. It was a yell rather than a thought. Let me try it over again. Is it rational to believe in a bad God? Anyway, a God so bad as all that? The Cosmic Sadist, the spiteful imbecile?

I think it is, if nothing else, too anthropomorphic...The picture that I was building up last night was simply the picture of a man like S. C. - who used to sit next to me at (college) dinner and tell me what he'd been doing to cats that afternoon. Now a being like S. C., however magnified, couldn't invent or create or govern anything. He would set traps and try to bait them. But he'd never have thought of baits like love, or laughter, or daffodil, or a frosty sunset. HE make a universe? He couldn't make a joke, or a bow, or an apology, or a friend.
(A Grief Observed, pp. 26-28)

Satan

There is a story of a man who was walking through Johannesburg, South Africa, one day, when he saw a figure sitting on a church step at the side of the street weeping.

As he got nearer he realised with some astonishment that it was the Devil. Despite some misgivings, he approached the figure and asked, "Excuse me but aren't you the Devil?" "Yes," the figure replied. "So you're actually Satan?" the man asked. "That's right," the figure sobbed. "But - in that case - why are you crying?" "It's these Christians," the Devil wept, "they blame me for everything!"

Satan plays no part in Jewish thought, but in some Christian theologies he plays a part verging on dualism - a good god and a bad god - which can lead to very depressing results. The film "A German Life" (2016) consists of an interview with an old lady of 103, Brunhilde Pomsel, who lived in Berlin during the war. She was politically naive and became a secretary in Goebbels Ministry of Propaganda. Her best friend Eva Löwenthal, who was Jewish, was killed in Auschwitz in 1945, and at the end of the war

Pomsel was imprisoned by the Russians for five years. At the end of the film, she says. *"God doesn't exist. But the Devil certainly does."*

In the book of Job, Satan, which means 'adversary', plays the part of a prosecuting counsel in the courtroom of heaven. He is a member of the Lord's, or Yahweh's, court though not a very attractive one. He is allowed to torment Job, but only within the limits laid down by the Lord himself. There is no ultimate division of responsibility.

In the New Testament the devil plays a far more active part. After his baptism, Jesus was pushed into the wilderness and was *"tempted by Satan"* (Mark 1.13). In the parable of the sower and four kinds of soil, Jesus explains: *"These are the ones on the path where the word is sown: when they hear, Satan immediately comes and takes away the word that is sown in them."* (Mark 4.15) When Jesus sent seventy (or seventy two) followers ahead of him, he said *"I watched Satan fall from heaven like a flash of lightning."* (Luke 10.21)

1 Peter 5.8, a regular reading in the service of Night Prayer, says *"Like a roaring lion your adversary the devil prowls around, looking for someone to devour."* And in the Letter to the Ephesians, the writer says, *"You were dead through the trespasses and sins in which you once lived, following the course of this world, following the ruler of the power of the air, the spirit that is now at work among those who are disobedient."* (Ephesians 2.1-2)

The concept of Satan came to have prominent place in some theologies, especially that of St Augustine, (354 - 430 AD), who ascribed the troubles of the world to "the Fall", the original disobedience of Adam and Eve in Genesis 3. But how could God allow temptation to come into a perfect world? The answer was that Satan had been an angel of light, but had rebelled against God and become his enemy, as described in the prophet Isaiah:

> *How you are fallen from heaven,*
> *O Day Star, son of Dawn!...*
> *You said in your heart,*
> *I will ascend to heaven*
> *I will raise my throne*
> *above the stars of God...*

> *But you are brought down to Sheol,*
> *to the depths of the Pit.*
> *(Isaiah 12, 13, 15)*

But, as is clear from verse 4, this is a poetic diatribe against the pride of the king of Babylon, not against some supernatural being.

I find the emphasis put on the Satan as a kind of negative God unhelpful. But this is not to deny the existence of evil on the spiritual as well as the human plane. The renowned psychiatrist, Carl Jung (1875 - 1961), wrote a letter in 1961 in which he said: *I am strongly convinced that the evil principle prevailing in the world, leads the unrecognized spiritual need into perdition, if it is not counteracted either by a real religious insight or by the protective wall of human community. An ordinary man, not protected by an action from above and isolated in society cannot resist the power of evil, which is called very aptly the Devil. But the use of such words arouse so many mistakes that one can only keep aloof from them as much as possible.*

In my years as vicar, I have occasionally been asked to pray in houses with some spiritual disturbance. Just praying Compline, (Night Prayer), in the place I have found surprisingly effective. As a very experienced exorcist, a monk said, "It's quite simple really. You say your prayers and the Lord deals with it."

There is for me a wise approach, which allows acceptance of a wide range of phenomena. In 'The Devils of Loudun' (1952) Aldous Huxley wrote,

If they ignore the call to union with the Son through works, if they forget that the final end of human life is the liberating and transfiguring knowledge of the Father, in whom we have our being, they will never reach their goal. For them there will no union with the Spirit; there will be a mere merging with spirit, with every Tom, Dick and Harry of a psychic world, most of whose inhabitants are no nearer to enlightenment than we are, while some may actually be more impenetrable to the Light than the most opaque of incarnate beings. (p. 84, chapter 3, Chatto & Windus)

Elihu for the Defence

By the time that Job and his three friends have gone through three cycles of arguments, the positions have not changed. Job refuses to invent a list of sins which would give God the excuse to unleash all these torments onto him:

> *As God lives, who has taken away my right,*
> *and the Almighty, who has made my soul bitter,*
> *I hold fast my righteousness, and will not let it go;*
> *my heart does not reproach me for any of my days.*
> (Job 27.2,6)

Eliphaz, Bildad and Zophar continue to insist on God's goodness and greatness, and the corresponding weakness and sinfulness of mankind.

> *Dominion and fear belong to God;*
> *he makes peace in his high heaven.*
> *How then can a mortal be righteous before God?*
> *How can one born of woman be pure?*
> *If even the moon is not bright*
> *and the stars are not pure in his sight,*
> *how much less a mortal, who is a maggot,*
> *and a human being, who is a worm!*
> (Job 25.2, 4-6)

Chapters 32 to 37 are the speech of a young man, Elihu, who takes it upon himself to set both Job and his friends right. It is widely accepted that these chapters were put in at a later date by a writer who was scandalised by what he saw as an inadequate defence of God. Unfortunately these six chapters add nothing to what has been said before.

Job is still accused of wickedness:
> *Of a truth, God will not do wickedly,*
> *and the Almighty will not pervert justice.*
> *Would that Job were tried to the limit,*
> *because his answers are like those of the wicked.*
> *For he adds rebellion to his sin;*
> *he multiplies his words against God.*
> (Job 34.36 -37)

God is still supreme power and supreme justice:
> *Of a truth, God will not do wickedly,*
> *and the Almighty will not pervert justice.*
> *Surely God is great, and we do not know him;*
> *the number of his years is unsearchable.*
> (Job 34.12, 36.26)

The point Elihu emphasises is the folly of arguing with God:
> *Surely God does not hear an empty cry,*
> *nor does the Almighty regard it.*
> *How much less when you say that you do not see him,*
> *that the case is before him and you are waiting for him!*
> (Job 35.13,14)

So, with Job and his three friends having argued themselves to the point of exhaustion, and the young man from Buz (in Arabia) adding nothing new, the stage is set for silence and a whirlwind out of which God speaks. Does this lead to a resolution?

God Speaks

Most commentators regard the Lord's, or Yahweh's, speeches as unsatisfactory; they simply do not address Job's complaints. Chapters 38 and 39 begin with the LORD asking Job a series of sarcastic questions:

> Who is this who darkens counsel by words without knowledge?
> Where were you when I laid the foundations of the earth?
> Have you commanded the morning, and caused the dawn to know its place?
> Can you bind the chains of the Pleiades, or loose the cords of Orion? etc. etc.

What is happening here? I think with the speeches of God we move from a philosophical or theological debate about the character of God to an actual encounter. The point is no longer an attempt to build an intellectual position which can answer life's mystifying questions, but to something like a mystical experience. And as this is a Jewish book, that experience must have ethical content.

In chapters 38 and 39 God describes the marvels of the natural world - the earth and sea, light and darkness, snow and hail, rain and ice, the constellations, clouds and lightning, lions and ravens, mountain goats and wild asses, wild oxen and ostriches, horses and hawks. God then challenges Job directly, who replies,

> *See, I am of small account: what shall I answer you?*
> *I lay my hand on my mouth.*
> (Job 40:2)

In chapters 40 and 41 God continues to put Job in his place, describing the hippopotamus (Behemoth)and crocodile (Leviathan) as if they were two mythical creatures. Job responds:

> *I had heard of you by the hearing of the ear,*
> *but now my eye sees you;*
> *therefore I despise myself,*
> *and repent in dust and ashes.*
> (Job 42:5-6)

Chapters 40 & 41 may have been added later. What is undeniable is the extraordinary power of the poetry of these four chapters. But how could they help Job?

The Natural World

Sometimes the fact of nature around us can bring a measure of healing.

George Bernard Shaw, a famous playwright and theatre critic in the first half of the twentieth century, was trying to comfort a woman friend whose husband had left her for another woman. She was in absolute bits. They were walking along the street at night under a sky full of stars. With great kindness, Bernard Shaw said, *"Look up, my dear, look up. There is more than this."*

Iris Murdoch, in her philosophy book "The Sovereignty of Good", wrote:

"I am looking out of my window in an anxious and resentful state of mind, oblivious to my surroundings, brooding perhaps on some damage done to my prestige. Then suddenly I observe a hovering kestrel. In a moment everything is altered. The brooding self with its hurt vanity has disappeared. There is nothing now but the kestrel. And when I return to thinking of the other matter it seems less important." (p.82)

Maybe there is a clue here.

Encountering God

Was it simply the experience of having a direct encounter with God that changed Job? Such is implied in our story. But what happens when we have such an encounter? Here are two stories, the first from Alcoholics Anonymous:

I cannot sleep. Suddenly a thought comes. Can all these worthwhile people I have known be wrong about God? Then I find myself thinking about myself and a few things I had wanted to forget. I begin to see that I am not the person I had thought myself… It is a shock.

Then comes a thought that is like a voice, **"Who are you to say there is no God?"** *It rings in my head. I can't get rid of it…*

Suddenly, I feel a wave of utter hopelessness sweep over me. I am in the bottom of hell. And there a tremendous hope is born. It might be true.

I tumble out of bed onto my knees. I know not what I say. But slowly a great peace comes to me. I feel lifted up. I believe in God. I crawl back into bed and sleep like a child.
(pp. 214-215)

The other story comes from "Face to Face" by Frances Young. Frances Young is a theologian and Methodist minister in Birmingham. Her first child, Arthur, was and is, severely handicapped. Face to Face tells her story. Half way through the book comes this passage:

It was not long after I had shared with the group that I had an experience which can probably be regarded as the fundamental breakthrough. It was only momentary, and I find it very difficult to place in terms of time of day or context in the life of the family. But I know precisely what chair I was sitting in, and that I was sitting on the edge of the chair, about to go off and do something or other around the house. It was one of those 'thought-flashes' that seem to have no context: **"It doesn't make any difference to me whether you believe in my reality or not."**

I had a sense of being stunned, of being put in my place. It is difficult to see why, really. It is after all a theological commonplace, and I do not think that I had thought for a very long time that my intellect could solve the problems. It was all so very ordinary, too. Nothing dramatic happened. I got up and got on with whatever I was going to do. I have not, however, seriously doubted the reality of God since that moment.
(p. 64)

I have had one similar experience. When I was around 30 I went on holiday to Lee Abbey, an Anglican holiday centre on the north coast of Devon near Lynton. It is a converted Victorian mansion (with a Victorian Gothic name), based on an earlier house "Lee Manor," the manor house of the Wichhalse family as described in 'Lorna Doone'. It was a Wednesday evening, when there was the usual devotional talk or epilogue. I cannot remember what was said, but it was unrelated to how disturbed I felt. I walked out into the night, along a level path leading to Jenny's Leap, a clifftop lookout. I can still see the lights of Swansea twinkling on the other side of the Bristol Channel, and the stars overhead. It was then that I exploded at God, and said, very loud, "Frankly, God, if I were able to choose between having you, and having enough money to give me security, **I'd choose the money!**" Instantly, rather like standing under a push-button shower (which doesn't exist) and being drenched in warm water, I was given faith. I walked back to the main house in joy. I learnt a very important lesson that night - that God can take anything we throw at him, our doubt and distrust and anger. The only thing he can't deal with is our masks.

I believe this is why in the book of Job, God says to Eliphaz:

> *My wrath is kindled against you and against your two friends;*
> *for you have not spoken of me what is right,*
> *as my servant Job has."*
> (Job 42.7)

It is also why Jesus said to the religious leaders in the Temple:

> *"Truly I tell you, the tax-collectors and prostitutes are going into the kingdom of heaven ahead of you."*
> (Matthew 21.31)

I suggest that what the book of Job aims to do is not to provide us with a solution, nor a resolution, but an invitation to an encounter with God.

What should we then do?

There is an insightful passage in the book by C. S. Rodd:

"Although Job saw only God the torturer, and the silence of the land of no return, he did two things: he refused to renounce his integrity, and he would not abandon prayer."
(The Book of Job p. 107)

It sums up the fundamental necessity of staying honest before God; not trying to be pious or good, but relating directly to God with all one's pain and rage, even when, especially when, you feel he has let you down.

Job's troubles come to an end when he forgives his friends.

> *"My servant Job shall pray for you, for I will accept his prayer not to deal with you according to your folly."...*
> *And the Lord restored the fortunes of Job when he had prayed for his friends, and the Lord gave Job twice as much as he had before. "*
> (Job 42:8,10)

AFTERWORD

The ending of Job sounds like a fairy tale, but at its heart is the spiritual truth that nothing cuts us off from God as quickly as resentment.

It is plain that a life which includes deep resentment leads only to futility and unhappiness... For when harbouring such feelings we shut ourselves off from the sunlight of the Spirit.
(Alcoholics Anonymous p. 66)

And Jesus himself warned,

> "If you forgive others their trespasses, your heavenly Father will also forgive you; but if you do not forgive others, neither will your Father forgive your trespasses."
> (Matthew 6.14-15)

When we have done that, all that is left is to get on with the ordinary business of living. When Archbishop Rowan Williams was asked in an interview how he coped with the overwhelming number of demands on him, he said, *"I try to do the next thing as carefully and prayerfully as I can."*

Whether in sorrow or joy, in prosperity or pain, we are called simply to live out our lives as carefully and prayerfully as possible, and continue to *"cultiver notre jardin."*

Bibliography

Introducing Job

in chronological order

H H Rowley	The Growth of the Old Testament (1950)
Gerhard von Rad	Old Testament Theology vol 1 (1957, trans, 1962)
ed. D Winton Thomas	Documents from Old Testament Times (1958)
A MacBeath	The Book of Job - a study manual (1966)
C Westermann	Handbook to the Old Testament (1967, trans 1969)
W H Schmidt	Introduction to the Od Testament (1979, trans 1984)
ed. R Alter. spec. M Greenberg	Literary Guide to the Old Testament (1987)

The Meaning of Job

The Bible

-	The Holy Bible (New Revised Standard Version)
Gerhard von Rad	Wisdom in Israel
Cyril S. Rodd	The Book of Job
H. H. Rowley	The Book of Job

Theology and Philosophy

-	Alcoholics Anonymous
Aldous Huxley	The Devils of Loudun
Alister McGrath	Christian Theology
Iris Murdoch	The Sovereignty of Good
John A Sanford	Evil - the Shadow Side of Reality
Ulrich Simon	Theology of Auschwitz
Philip Yancey	Where is God When it Hurts?
Voltaire	Candide

Personal Experience

-	Alcoholics Anonymous
Philip Halle	Lest Innocent Blood be Shed
C. S. Lewis	A Grief Observed
Frances Young	Face to Face

AFTERWORD

www.ingramcontent.com/pod-product-compliance
Lightning Source LLC
Chambersburg PA
CBHW071007080526
44587CB00015B/2372